SUNDAY The Game

Cassia Cassitas

SUNDAY The Game

2nd Edition

2013

Original Title: Domingo O Jogo

Translation: Fal Vitielo

Cover: Allacriativa

http://cassiacassitas.com.br

ISBN: 978-85-915328-7-2

B120 – Theory of Knowledge

"Love builds bridges where there are none."

R.H. Delaney

Acknowledgements

Literature is a wonderful friend. It speaks when we want to listen. It waits for the right moment to show its presence. It ensnares us with one line, its title. It does not deny us information. It tirelessly teaches so much to so many. It respects our timeline, never getting offended with our forgetfulness, repeating the answers to our questions as many times as we need. Even using the same words, it may take different connotations. It shows us surprising new configurations of familiar elements, helping us to write a better unfolding to our lives.

All my gratitude to my family, who has always listened to me, no matter what words I used, as authors of works that presented different worlds to me — possible lives, distinct dimensions and other possibilities for action and expression.

Thank you.

Preface

Those who pass us by, do not go alone, do not leave us alone; they leave a little piece of themselves; they take a little piece of us.

Antoine de Saint-Exupéry

Sunday, the Game is an invitation to an adventure, to a strategy to a game played on any given Sunday, at every Sunday dinner — where the reader is the main character, the strategist. While reading, developing tactics of self-actualization, dilemmas and conflicts are faced and a final victory of understanding is achieved.

With this musing modality of learning, the reader perceives his place in space and time, in the world — in this globalized, post-modern, mechanistic world, full of technologic novelties, people get involved with these tools of modernity in such a way that they start to live automatically, reproducing patterns, without knowing why; without thinking or reflecting: Why live?

It is the poetic-philosophical understanding of how much our culture values and exacerbates individualism and competition, without taking the time to retrieve family values and their behavioral significance.

In this unique book, the author Cassia Cassitas presents her theory of human knowledge, based on relationships between the individual and the family, from the perspective of a dynamic board game where pieces of the self are moved - a game full of metaphors.

All this takes place on the free day, the universal day of reflection, Sunday — from sunrise to sunset, and each reading brings the game anew, a new surge of hope. Everyone can remake their paths; earn new victories, scores more points.

It is possible to go through this book for the simple pleasure of reading it, or playing with it: reinforcing self- esteem as the pages go by; enhancing a sense of sharing, of union, while developing skills and trust.

However, as the Brazilian sociologist Paulo Freire once said, "Men don't learn only with their intelligence, but also with their body and guts, their sensitivity and imagination". Readers are then invited to live and understand the experience, since while playing they simulate situations and through them they reach valuable insights.

The reader, while critically analyzing at the deepest of levels, becomes involved in the Game, finding solutions to daily life — as we can say, using Carl Rogers' words, a "living learning" happens, and its characteristic is that of being "full of meaning".

With every new page, Sunday, the Game brings a wide array of possibilities, revolutionizing the existence of those who surrender to it body and soul.

Henrique Chagas
Author and editor of
www.verdestrigos.org

Contents

PART III - CONFIGURATION OF THE GAME

PART IV - THE GAME

PART V - THE END OF THE GAME

Part I

The player, the strategy and the result

Introduction

Thousands of lives have linked their directions to games. The ancient glyph of a board, similar to a tic-tac-toe grid, was found in pre-historic caves in Warscheueck, Austria, and in a cave in Fontainebleau, France. The human being is fascinated by games, by the dispute, by the binomial "victory and defeat". At the same time they wish to win, humans enjoy watching failure, other people's failure.

This is what this book is about; a game, full of strategies, with the sole intent to win. As you read it, you are invited to participate in the competition, to take your turn, which will determine the final results.

Everyone is a player in this game. But you are the star, the favorite competitor; it is to you, the reader, that all the secrets will be revealed. It is you who will be trained to succeed. You are the captain of the team, the owner of the game.

You, the main character, will learn about the matches' peculiarities — that it can be individual or collective, and there is no maximum number of participants. In this game, there is a place for men, women, fears, ideologies, certainties and changes of paradigm. Anything can happen.

Sunday is a symbol of free time, without plans or obligations. It brings to the surface feelings of freedom. It brings to the mind the repose of the warrior; alternatives; pleasant activities. In the game of life what is of significance is the position that one occupies, or would like to occupy.

In the freedom of Sunday, dreams become real defining the stage of the fray. If the desired end does not match reality, what does it matter?

The construction starts in the mind. Everything comes from individual strategies, but evolves towards collective perception. Some secret inner animal locked up until that moment — like an unknown love — moves across the board, constructing the world, planning the future.

But events do not determine the players' moves. On the contrary, it's the players that determine the events; and that is what is of consequence. To play, to take control of your Sunday, requires nerve. It is for women who let their hair down, for men who look each other in the eye. You, the main character, awaken to the awareness that the game is advancing - evolving like life itself. There is no going back, because in an instant dinner has ended, it is over.

Dinner is the start, it is the field of confrontation, the demarcation of territories and the place of supply — re- nourishing the soul and the five senses with the nutrients we need to survive, the weapons with which we will fight; it is our health, our strength and ideally our pleasure.

Many are the stages where opportunities coexist with adversity, where we expand our capacity to observe, to act — sometimes changing, other times accepting. Only the wisest know the right time to stand, to overcome, to transform, and in the end to bless and celebrate.

Soon, everyone is gone. Everything is done. The possibilities have become past; the present is in the mirror and the future is left for the next round.

Family is the root. It brings life and is life. It is wisdom much greater than human knowledge, inherent in every player's family — necessary, essential, vital to development and learning. Our family — families united by blood, by contract, by solitude, united by common interests — the family we have, the one we desire, the one we once had, is everywhere. It is in the movies, in the streets, in the bakery, in the park, in the church, in the books. It is impossible to ignore it, especially on Sundays.

With it come all the feelings that take hold of us at the simple mention of the word "family". Its marks are left on the surface of our skin, in the way we walk and sit, how we hold our knife and fork, how we avoid confrontation. It permeates the soul, streams down the skin, searching for other eyes, other orbs, willing to look at the walking revelation of our character, screaming its truths with every movement — pleading for love, searching for completion.

The moments of greatest joy or sadness are shared by the family.

All families are "normal". Within every family, there are essential role models — examples of what to do, and what not to do, examples of great love, of great challenge, of profound pain. The family is witness to every faltering and new beginning. It is within the family that the greatest mistakes are made and the best decisions taken.

There are moments when all the garbage carried in our pockets and in our hearts is put out onto the sidewalks for everyone to see. These are the daily provisions of our lives, the stuff we are made of, which has nurtured us until this moment. We carry these things within us, whether we like it or not, until we decide to stop and examine each of them — these little preciosities, treasures, "nonsenses". Those who pass by are able to see the diverseness — realize that we can say no to the world, reshape our own image choose something at variance.

Through the scars left by pains caused or suffered, we acquire a more flexible view of the world. We develop an ability to accept the imperfections of others and ourselves. But there comes an unbearable need to action that explodes in an urgency of movement — and if not exercised or manifested, gives rise to illness. Acting and breathing, this is the only way to survive.

Whenever we make the right decisions, we are able to see how powerful the effect of action is — how important it is to participate, to speak out, to do — with love and reflection - and before, during and after, to feel the power flowing in every word, warming the hands, exhausting the muscles of the effort.

Our family and their behavior — the great exemplars, present in even the simplest of situations — shape the very bearing of our lives; even influencing the weight of our rhetoric, making us assertive or proud — though not always altering our blood pressure.

However, there is much more to this that is essential to all our answers — that it is the acceptance and denial of the opportunities which present themselves to us every day, every minute — blessing the players — for they have given us all that they had to give — this is the starting point of the true quest — the searching for what we want, for what we can become. The objective of all training is to prepare the player, motivating him to assume his position.

To be ready.

When we look at the years in retrospect, there is so much to learn — to avoid; to repeat and to celebrate, the challenges that have become stories — the unplanned achievements, which only happened because we were not thinking — at that moment, we simply had believed, dreamed.

When we turn our eyes to the youngest, born of another world, at another time, in other circumstances, we observe avenues which were opened in our lifetime through our discoveries — which in spite of all our efforts, were not enough to overcome the immensity of what was unknown — at some point new possibilities arose, occasions kept materializing, replacing old certainties, creating still other realities. And we are still playing the game.

It is your trajectory that this book emphasizes, dear reader. You, the star player, have accessed information; you had set up the strategies utilizing heightened perceptions, outlining a life of actions and decisions centered on yourself. But, beware. To keep one's individuality does not mean to remain alone. Our extended selves multiplied through our children, deeds and friends, carry elements of our own existences. These are pieces of ourselves in others, pulsing through roots whose sap we sense circulating in the consequences of what we have been, dreamed and done. This is now "collectively" our turn.

It is our turn to contribute so that others are able to say yes or no to these possibilities, to harvest these results;

to celebrate, love and work; to work with diligence. Though our lives are but instances it is humanity itself that is transcendence.

Some lives are defined by a single instant, an attitude taken at some mundane event; raising a child; producing a report; cooking for another; walking.

The realization of any individual nature is only worthwhile if it creates a thought that helps us to be more complete, more fulfilled, more ready for blessedness. This is what makes a good "game", and to this purpose there are the trainers, guides — the family.

Redraw the blueprint. Discover your treasures. Recover your skills. Embrace your family and bless them all. May your "game" be a good one.

Playing

With every birth, comes a new player, a "bundle of hope". We are all predestined to live witnessing this fascinating "game" of the world; some when still young, others later.

Discovering that dreams are nothing more than possibilities is one of the greatest realizations of our existence — to hold the dice and roll them, rationally or impulsively, for therein lies the key to the strategy — how to make real something that, somewhere, already exists, that has already been dreamed of — by acknowledging our nature as a player, as one always wanting more.

The player is the person who advances by passing the baton. Sometimes it is the youth, other times it is the elder — but the player may choose boldness, self-assuredness, or the inexperience of youth — it may however choose the veteran with his knowledge, certainty or weariness as the choice. The adult is always ready to take the helm, to take control of the action with "wisdom", conviction and all the baggage accumulated along the way.

A youth, however may leap from childhood, take the reins of the moment, break the established order of the world, and in an enduring childlike nature ignore the possible consequences of failure and be unhesitant in the face of danger.

A player will need both of these qualities to advance — sometimes the child does not act in time; other times, the adult arrives too late. It is essential to provide the player with all that is necessary so that the child can survive until the end of the game and the grown up has the strength, determination and opportunity to apply what it has already learned. The combining of all this is an alchemy requiring wisdom.

Knowledge, training and respect, fused and blessed with the capacity of empathy — that is putting oneself in another person's shoes, feeling what they feel, seeing what they see, understanding their decision making process is the "wisdom of character" which this book and you will construct simultaneously.

Over the course of many Sundays, you will wake up with different mind sets, at different stages of your life, and will have received all the training necessary to utilize the state of things to your advantage. Do not expect ready answers, only opportunities and perspectives. This is what transforms the player into a winner, a champion.

The "dream" is the aim, the reason for the journey, the final goal. It is the prize that the player hopes to achieve at the end of this contest. It is the scent of victory, the taste of consecration. It is each and everyone's raison d'être. It does not matter how bright or colorful another's dream may seem, it will never be as satisfying as the realization of our own — so deeply rooted in our memory, built upon our educations and inspired by still unfulfilled needs. Focus on your dream, define it, give it time and attention, for it belongs to you — the "star player", the main character.

In this "game", everything is an expression of you. It is up to you to define the configuration of the board, to determine the families' structure, to establish its limits. It is up to you to decide the players and their circumstances; to assign to other players, members of your family, the roles to which you think that they are best suited — static, without reaction; dynamic, meddling with facts; passive, merely responding to the moves made by you, the "star" player.

Who comes to play? The father, whose voice cannot be described merely with his words, for in his tone, is everything he has to say — the words do not make it clearer? The loving mother, who embraces us with her eyes, our feelings becoming Olympian when she gives us her attention? And what about the children — how many are there? They recognize us as their fortress; they leave for the world, but always return. Are there brothers or sisters, those who know the subtleties of the "game?" Are there grandparents, who come and go, cousins and uncles? Aunts are the best.

Everyone takes their turn. It does not matter if they do well or poorly. One day, they also awaken full of dreams, making plans. They too are players with their own strategies. Very early on, they took possession of the place they occupy in our lives and have never left. They move according to their own natures, their values, their beliefs. They are loyal to who they truly are. This is the only way we advance — by taking the helm; commanding our own destinies, taking our own steps.

In their game, we are not the "star" player, the main character. This is why they may become our masters in the art of winning. Some are experts in resilience — others specialists in commanding. There are those who are always searching in a seemingly endless war, for only God knows what. Battle after battle they are warriors.

Every lesson is precious keeping us focused on the "dream" which, while awake, we seek to create — and reveal.

The role of supporting actor in other people's lives makes us ready to play our own game, to heighten our own senses in the face of new opportunities. To face them assertively, we need to observe the context, the environment and the position of the players who present them — to know their world, their ideas and eventually to reach an answer. This is the move. The strategy consists in how to make it.

Strategy is thought, observation, a calculated action to generate a fact. One cannot develop a strategy with flowers; it is necessary to use bricks and cement, with every block shaped, fitted and organized to reach an end. During the narrative of the episodes, you are invited to establish your own strategy. On the board, victories and failures happen, mixed with doubts, producing changes. Sometimes, wars are waged internally. Sleeping hurts.

There is so much thirst for victory that the will to win tightens your chest, pulls you away from your comfort zone and throws you into a new perspective, another context. When this happens, the meaning of predetermined result is inevitably altered. The importance of the "wish" is questioned and reshaped.

Sometimes, nothing, almost nothing seems to change. We simply follow the initial route, with the same certainties, the same values and the same ideals. Nevertheless, between challenges and repetitious behavior, the game continues changing the way of being and living of the participants unaware and without asking their permission. If, however you are ready, you will be able to identify these moments and rewrite your strategies. You will check what is inside your inner backpack, making the best of the space available. In the makings of success, there is no place for embellishments. There is sincerity and transparency, mainly internal; this is the material which the "star" player will collect during training.

The central challenge is playing to maximize, minimize and change. If the right combinations are made, you will achieve whatever you want. To play is to be alive, considering the moves of all participants advancing and progressing.

But the book also has its strategies. To get to the next stage, with the entire necessary arsenal, there are results to be collected — added to the compendium of data after every episode described. Some others must be discarded along the way. There are strategies used to awaken dormant elements, tools to explore the dark caves waiting for light to illuminate — daily repetitions which become imperceptible, but exist and intervene with the mundane. All the elements, listed as results, need to be understood — this is the training of the senses in the encounter of "dinner." This is what it means to be ready.

When the emphasis of the narrative is in training, you will receive guidance. A state of mind will be refined; the fashioning of a winner. In the same way, as you become conscious, the narrative will include facts, memories, and feelings. Written in the first person singular, it is you who feels, remembers and does.

The final outcome will be determined by the combination of all answers, objectives and results. Establish one of these for yourself and read the book, searching for it, as if you were arming yourself for a day of work with ideas, desires, emotions and actions, planned so as not to make a commitment to the next step or get involved with fashion. And then, build the world around you.

Part II

A Champion's training

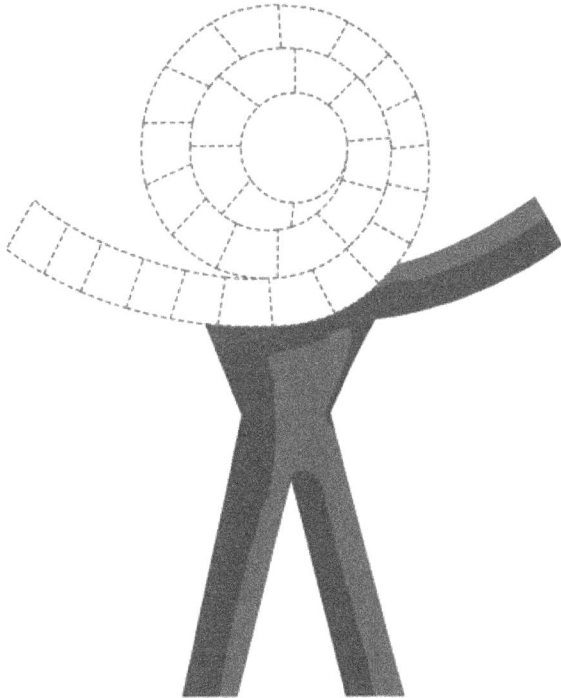

Before Waking Up

Every champion's victory starts with an honest conversation with the mirror. This Sunday, you will wake up and look at yourself. Examine your hair, your skin, your fingers. When you are ready, you will look in your own eyes and ask yourself: what do you want?

Each player is further ahead of the others in one or another aspect. Since they are really good at that, they are prepared. What are your skills? How can you use them to do what you really need to do?

What are you doing?

Your own fear reminds you of every precaution you need to take. Somewhere deep inside of you, the answer is waiting to be heard.

What are you afraid of?

You must carefully awaken and free yourself of your apprehensions. One by one — step by step. Come on, wake up. Your time has come. Your trainers are waiting for you to have "dinner".

Waking Up

Thanks you for listening to me. I really like talking. Sometimes it is all I want to do. Let out all the things inside my head, stuck in my throat — ideas, discoveries, questionings, everything is ready to be set free. This so-called "internal life" has its ups and downs, and according to the foods I eat, the books I read or the party I go to, this internal play is often intense. Sometimes, a comment, a gesture, a note in the newspaper, a song, anything is enough to accelerate it.

There're a lot of light, colorful rays of light. The light overwhelms me, gets out of control, and challenges the boundaries of the space I am willing to give it — it invades my ears. When I become cognizant, it is in my words. I wonder if this happens to everyone.

The light, this energy, has its own flow, its own trajectory. It goes wherever it wants, does what it wants without consent. I feel like a piece in a puzzle, an element in a design. And the most intriguing thing is that as I recognize myself as its cause, I lose it. It is as if the control of this "irreverence" has always been with me, but when I practice with it, if I exercise influence over it, try to control it, it burns out — extinguishes itself. At the same time that it submits to my control, to what I say, hear or do, it stops shining. Even though controlled, it continues to be present, but more as a shadow, matted and doubtful — it becomes a question.

This light moves, warms, arouses me. It gives me impetus and courage. I feel like singing, running, whirling, flying, making things happen. My soul wants to dance. As if there was a spotlight pointed at the center of my being. It is power.

To be powerful is to be alive. Life is power. Life desires to be the master of your time. Wherever I am now, could I take possession of it? What should I do with my share of it? Does everyone think about this?

I read once that someone asked Saint Augustine what God had made of His time before creation. The answer was simple. It was God who created time. In his studies, based on his questionings about life, Saint Augustine defended not only that time was part of creation, but also that it is finite — it had a beginning and will have an end. Should I wait until my time is over, in this waking dream?

Such rays of light make me tremble, and at these moments, I remember the rain — the lightning announcing the thunder. Could a storm be coming into my life? The days of torment unite the thunder and light. The light spreads out, and while it hypnotizes, the thunder enters, shaking certainties. How can one hold on to the ruins, of what ceased to be? I think I like noise.

After the storm, the rainbow; the sun; the light again, coming through the window insisting on waking me. We can always rewrite our desires, people say. To dream again… to dream anew. The same dream, in a new way — forgetting the idea of claiming ownership. It does not let me sleep. The light is mine, is yours, and belongs to the world. Through the window, it illuminates the chaos, calls me out to life. Even on Sundays? It wants me to be in charge and it pushes me into the choices, goals, strategies and results that I want for myself. It flows and involves me, keeping the focus lit-up, outlining the construction. Blessed.

I am getting up. I am going to have "dinner."

•••

**light
shadow
storm**

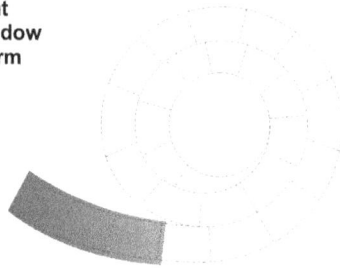

player's age

It is always worth it to turn on the lights and illuminate, because there is a lot to be lost when the answers are not clear or in perspective. Possible disconnections between pieces which seem not to fit are due to the self-omissions in front of the mirror, rather than the work of the mentors. The answers are there.

When one knows their own situation, it is possible to control fate, to survive the storms, to illuminate one's focus, moving towards the light.

The Awareness of Life

You need to observe, to be aware of the reality surrounding you, to get ready to coexist with other people's choices. Diversity is a fact. From the differences between people, come the greatest of constructive victories, synthesize — to imagine that this difference should be fought against and exterminated is to lose half of the story. It is like flattening the land, cutting off the trees, reducing everything to dirt.

The family that educates us needs to make difficult choices in taking this training even further; finding out where the best results happen, investing in them; sometimes discovering talents, other times improving weaknesses; detecting and eliminating the wastes of energy in all its aspects; concentrating on skills; and preventing damaging dilemmas from entering the spirit.

This is how a winner is educated — developing their eyes, ears and the capacity to make decisions. In a less known world, the natural growth, almost vegetative, would be enough; but with globalization and the digitalization of life, forget about it. Now one needs to train for the "high bar."

Like a grain of sand

It is morning. The sun is shining. I need to wake up, to open my eyes and get up. The house is silent. The table is not set. There is no smell of coffee. The clothes are where I left them last night. Outside, the world has kept on going. The day is ready. Only I have stopped. I am everything. Everywhere I look there are traces of me, signs and secrets spread around the house — in a world that is only mine.

I am alone and I need to learn. Learn. Learn. Learn. Could this be my lot in life? Getting out of bed, lifting my soul —   opening my eyes, my mind; the window, the coffee pot — watching the grinds dissolve and feeling the smell of coffee fill the air. Listening to my own thoughts and breathing. Looking for what I have kept in the drawers, what I once considered important. Rubbing my eyes, welcoming what the day brings. Setting the table and changing the seating arrangement. Redrawing the lines and moving the secrets, as if they were grains of sand in the desert of mankind.

I need to learn to be a grain and to see other grains — a man among other men. To build castles, to observe, to mingle — to hold hands; to call; to breathe the sea air; to absorb; to touch and to feel — to let myself determine the way. To preserve my identity, in spite of the difference and even in the indifference — to soak; to take; to stay; to move; to shape my destiny with every detail of the day — to be like rust, to set free, to bury the shell softly despite it all and without pain — yet, in the pain, to become a pearl. Getting up with the warming sun, the sun that melts, nurtures, burns, connects. A grain in the soil, unique — absolute.

I need to learn to be sand. I need to fly with the wind, following the path of my world; to fly according to my own pre-destinations, towards that part of the world that attracts me and is mine, that I accept and choose as real; to quench my thirst and open my eyes; to have roots; to be concrete; to build a house; and to be light enough not to miss the wind — to fly again.

A grain of sand is so small. I like small people, elderly people, big people; people without a group, who think they are alone; people who laze upon the ground and see only the desert; people who forget to open their eyes, to see the immensity around them; people who are cast asides, who choose to be free — unique, malleable, ardent — as desert and heat; the kind of people who hide their knowledge in silence — who silence their thoughts until their intentions are clear; a human being, clear and whole growing towards immensity opening his arms and his mind, holding the wind, in a euphoric hug.

Profound, immense, sand — I want the clamor of the stage, of the audience. I want to live, until every scintilla of life in me has drained and I've become desert. To breathe the way; to be alone and whole; to reach the strand; to disappear, leaving a breeze behind — I passed, and I was a shadow, or a breeze. Me.

With every wave, I absorb the sea. With every shift of the wind, I let myself be embraced by life, incorporating in silence the roads which come and go; I open my eyes and see, for a fraction of a second. I look at the scars; the objects in the drawer; the empty table; the bread; the waves; the beach; the shells; the sand; the wall; the house; the desert; the sea; the mountains; the grains of sand — my brothers. To recover my path, this is my triumph.

I feel very deeply, with such intensity to receive the

world and to know love, to know myself; to clean out my closet and after, to explore myself; to define my voice; to coexist with truths that ignore the light; to search for answers to my questions; to open drawers; to speak, without judgment; to accept the time, the mood, the tumor; to learn how to be me in the world, provoking and invoking; to coexist, without the hurry to produce or shine — without the pain of the idea that is gone — of the actions that did not materialize — what will be left for another generation to do; to live; to create.

Today, I will be happy.

•••

family
influences
world

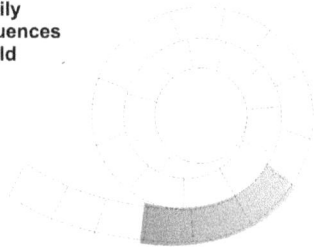

a place in the world

To see the light — beyond your own veins; to speak

openly, to argue and debate, to make things happen according to your view. After all, you are the "star" player, the owner of the table.

Divergence, disagreement and contestation are not created, but learned at home, at school, during childhood. Some of your attitudes and qualities may cause admiration; others, contempt. It is at this point that it is always possible to take the next step, to confront what you see, to cultivate what you admire — or to castigate yourself for feelings of incompetence, seeking reclusion, denying yourself the next undertaking.

It is necessary to live and remember as children do that if they are not good at something, they soon find other interests, things they like and things they are able to do. They assume their individuality and explore the world around them. They become like sand and let other grains join them. They roll in it, getting dirty, marking their time in words and scenes, writing in their souls the paths of self-achievement.

Childhood

Very early on, we learn how leaders behave in the everyday world of childhood, from the holding of cutlery, to the asking for the reason why the sky is blue. We find these out.

Some children are tireless teachers; they use all their encounters to evaluate and reinforce values. They seek to build everyone's self-confidence. They act with honesty and clarity. That is how they are made. They seem always to be an example to others. They assume the risk.

Others show the courage to have a relationship with people more evolved than they are; children who make them feel worse than everybody else, even when everyone sees them as the best in class. They know that if they acted as if they had all the words, all the facts and all the answers, they would be squandering the necessary elements to support the success of others. They are trainers in training.

The spark of leadership makes greatness arise in the

actions, in the emotions, in the personality of a winner. Using uniqueness, surprising language, while defining the surrounding energy and establishing starting points, he clarifies the available colors and the path to follow, adding to the environment the voice of persuasion, the color of arguments and a true feeling of fascination.

The Neighbors' Jabuticabas

Kneeling on the bed to open the window, while the morning comes in a yellow light, I realize it is today. They have already started. Today is the day. I can see the moment. It has arrived.

I love this day. I will sit outside and bathe in golden light. The backyard is red. My legs are thin. Among so many memories, this is the one which takes me back to when I was eight. I love waking up as a child. Will they take long?

I wear striped socks, giving myself a blue and orange importance, and find my crayons. Discreetly, I sit on the doorstep, playing with something, just to take a look. How many are there? Three. There are normally three. They are calm, quiet, almost subdued in their silence. Even their laughter is low. And their hair, soft and dark as the jabuticaba berries they pick. They do not wear crazy hairdos. I realize they are like rays of light — they like what they do, and that is why they shine. They never noticed, but I was humming all the time.

They spend the whole morning there. Time goes by. Dinner time comes and we have to wait for the afternoon. Time is theirs; they are in no hurry. They follow a colorful, light rhythm. They move like the sap of life, like a tree, for their own satisfaction. I come and go, occupying myself here and there. In my anxiety, I look up and see that enormous sky, all blue, telling me from above to wait, not to hurry — to be a child and not to worry? I wonder if there will be any jabuticaba berries left for us.

There always is. We have a mutual agreement, the first one I remember. We almost never talk. On this day of the year, they ask us for the pink bowl and return it full of jabuticaba. You know, I have never noticed if there are jabuticaba berries for sale. For me, they have always been a synonym for neighbors, for a green day; an explanation about ownership, rights, respect, and solidarity — after all, the jabuticaba tree is theirs. But we are children. For us, there are different rules, reasons, values, embarrassments. The branches invade our backyard. They come from the brown trunk that is on their land. Sometimes it is so easy; you just have to stretch your arm and pick a purple jabuticaba berry, but I have never done that. The trunk has always been an imperative, establishing a distance. The wall and the moss have a pact, and we respect it. The relation has never been disturbed.

If no one let us have a taste from the bowl, perhaps I would have a different opinion on this tricky subject. But they have never segregated the harvest, and have never considered themselves to be the only ones who deserved it. They have always distributed a part, good enough to satisfy us, to make us feel grateful. There, in that backyard, I learned the flavors and the colors of what was right and wrong — the difference between "I want" and "I must".

I still have doubts today. Would the jabuticaba berries have tasted so good, if bought and not received as a gift? I used to love those days.

In the backyard, they have other kinds of fruit. I have, too. But the other green branches did not invade our backyard. In my mind, the division between the colorful fruit on the other side of the wall and the dark jabuticaba berries — purple and black — was clear. We never got bowls with other fruit. I never wanted them. Would that be because we did not see them grow?

It must have been really good to stay up there,

because they used to spend hours and hours in the ritual, and their satisfaction was visible. They did not worry about the day passing by, a day bright now. They picked, played, ate. I wonder if they ever, for a single day, thought of inviting us to go up and touch the green.

Actually, now I know some go up, while some others just want to do it. There are studies about this. And they show, with words and colors, that everyone could do it; those who do not are making a choice. There are no invitations; there are only initiatives. They understand color.

We can also leave our inconspicuousness and climb. The branches are on our side; bunches of fruit sway gently in our backyard. It is not their scent, after all. It is the scent of the wind, which has set it free, the inattentive boy has carelessly thrown the fruit on the ground. To break the unspoken pact, however, it would be necessary to accept the results. They could enjoy our presence, allow and even share the laughter on the branches we claimed as ours. Or not; they could simply cut them, without pleading or smiling. Who would risk slipping on the wall and changing the course of things?

They really know about jabuticaba, the trees are full

of fruit. How sweet they are. I want to go there. There are days when that tree seems to be planted in me, every branch of it. And even though everything seems to be ready, they watch the color. They have learned to identify forms, sizes, textures. To seize the moment and make the decision, with gestures, thoughts, what I see now, all else is only movement. The harvest was abundant and good. They knew what they were doing. They had the skill.

So good. To notice the day, feel the moment, wait, watch unobserved. Small things that go deep inside me, silent like a root, as if I was just another fruit surrounded by others, waiting for my turn. What matters is the vibrant joy that I can still feel today. My legs seem to be thinner, the red backyard under my feet and the pink bowl in my hands. The heart beats like a green leaf, pushed and pulled. Everything is still there — an immense feeling; it passes through leaves, roots, reason. I smell its scent.

If a word is a memory, a remainder or a part, what does it matter? It is easy to change a golden delight into a grayish lament, but why, if the taste of the fruit is so sweet? The blacked- out minute is limited and perennial; we saw it pass, yet we did not fill it in. Is it really necessary to judge, to define, to label and to understand, to savor it? It is the jabuticaba that I miss.

Yes. They took a long time — hours. And I could only wait, because the hands were theirs. The person who works is the one who sets the rhythm; they take the steps, order the menu. Soon, we will have dinner.

•••

values
trainers
childhood

Sunday

Once in a while, the mentors need to sow other seeds, but most of the time they only have to nurture them and watch them grow.

The Pain

Truth has a price. Not by chance are we raised since our childhood to spare others sadness and pain — not to say everything or to lie a little is considered to be a kindness; it does no harm. But the rule does not apply when it comes to us. The lack of honesty about the self is the greatest of the small traps you can fall into. It stops us from having brilliant ideas. It reduces the speed of cognition and reaction. It devastates anyone's potential to achieve.

This is the time to prime for success. Be honest. A wish list can be useful to balance the possible and the impossible. Who are you?

Starting from the image reflected in the mirror, you can eradicate the devastating attitudes and thoughts that exhaust energy and paralyze action. Our champions in training have a broom in their hands, sweeping away everything that is harmful. Afterwards, they polish what is of good. It is time to eliminate all the excess ballast in the luggage of their memory.

It is very possible that from this activity, resentments will arise. But better than anyone else, you, the favorite in this game, are able to understand your own reasons and deliberate the course of action.

It is time to plan what is necessary to achieve your victory; the moment demands that you stop and choose; making space in your luggage, choices about people, behaviors and conclusions.

Beware. Do not fall into the frequent trap of trying to be everything to everyone all the time. Reasons and desires must be so clear that if you wake up in the middle of the night, you will still be able to answer as to where you are going, even half-asleep. Truth is the winning hand.

Rebellion

What am I going to wear? Whatever I am and like. I look in the wardrobe. I search for truths. It is difficult.

There is some dust which covers portraits, blurs the mirror. So much pain; my back hurts, my feet, my eyes. I feel like rain — thunder as anger, lightning as memories that haunt me; the whole night crying and now the dawn that insists on bringing light to a new day. Light. That should be comforting, but that makes me shiver, taking away my peace and my sleep. I just want to sleep, to rest, to forget the pain. To hibernate. Let me sleep and I will forget about dying.

This is the only way I can stand the light — until time sweeps away the discomfort and brings a brighter light — and a new day comes to be lived. What will they think if they see I love life so much?

Thinking is simple. Talking is easy. And how easy it is to talk without thinking. Men and women walk the streets wearing their beliefs. They think they reflect, in the eyes of those who see them, the image of what they are; what they have been; what they want to become — if they kept their intentions fresh; as if their dedications were not written on yellowed pages of days gone by. More pulsing existences wounded, as if they acted against the undertow that carries their bodies away. They float among memories, mirrors and dreams.

What about me? What to wear? It is Sunday. What is the right color? I do not know. The image oscillates. Certainties are few. Visions of what I think and am — half-memories, mirrors; chance, sport, religiosity? Should I choose patience or impulsivity? There are those who put their energy in their looks; a language to tell the world what they want. Sometimes, what they want; other times, what they should want. What do I want? Anesthetics. Something to help me stand the pain, stop feeling it. No more pain.

Why so much anguish? Why so much ardor? So much to do, to have, to be. What does man want after all? Immortality in one action; happiness in one passion; redemption in eternity; salvation, at the price of modernity; that the centuries may pass and the essence of love may prevail; to be a warrior; to avoid "the error;" to watch; to look carefully; and to let the image teach you and learn how to want.

Time goes by and fashion changes. It is forgotten. And it is in a hurry, because it gets old. Not love. Love gets under the skin of those who know it. It does not hurry; it never gets lost; it only accrues. At its essence, it changes into life and takes the world; it evaporates; rides the wind and goes to the Himalayas — imagine. It goes far, far away from me, far from the mind, the eyes and the body, without borders, lovers or chains. I have thought of being an animal; living with the wind, feeding off the sun; having water, a home, time; running, eating, sleeping; and waking up rested, without pain — human or inhuman, according to belief, leaving the rest to chance.

No more wanting. It reminds me of the elderly, with pockets full of minutes and a yearning soul. There is no desire. Is that the reason why one loses strength? I do not want to die, to undo myself. To want. Where is it?

Recklessness or charm, frustration or liveliness, what invented all this? Chance? What do I do with so many chances? Tie them around my neck or wear them on my feet? Tie them around my waist or exchange them for glasses? Not today. Judged and labeled, forbidden and freed, this Sunday, opinions are forgotten.

I want to love peace; to make a mess; to laugh; to live with light in the light; to get warm just thinking of going back; to carry; to play; to kiss and even to fight; to spin, and always land on my own feet; to be grounded, feet on the ground, following a schedule at work, doing things out of love; being active and modern; to reason; to be in a good mood; to be capable, bold, productive, proactive, fascinating, intelligent. What else?

It is too much. It is tiring. It hurts, all this "I have to". I get tired because I do not want it. This is not my zeitgeist. I look for a hand to hold, to help me stand. I want to share — or let go, let myself dissolve — to break free and disappear — to overflow, to run down, to grow — without the bitterness of so much passion; dispersed; diluted. My hands are not enough to be of service. Let them be me.

None of this will interfere with me. It will be me, from head to feet. I will dress myself of me. I will believe what the mirror tells me. Choose my colors, my steps and my shoes. Until I have the understanding, I will go through stages, follow the course, becoming stronger. Find the words to say thanks. No more fear. I open my eyes, set the colors free. Nothing is beige. How can you be happy with beige? It is Sunday. I will be red, yellow — purple and white. Black jeans, jeans go with everything.

I want to be like children and their soft hands; to nurture the muscles; to feel the blood; to choose my burden; the backpacks; to share what is inside them, without so much suffering; to awake from the tiredness, from the sleep, from the constant escape; to wash the face, the eyes, the pain; to clear the mind; to discover I am a survivor; to be human and to like this fact. Where are the children?

Today, I want everything; the fulfillment of being alive; to walk; to eat; to speak; even to be silent. I will meet my own needs, hear myself. And I promise to think before I speak, to give my full attention to the "essence"; to dedicate all my energy to its service. I open my eyes to myself to break the chains and dilate the mind — no borders of consciousness, and I welcome you with dignity, whoever you are. I do not care about age, weight or the color of your socks.

Today, I will be my guest of honor, in my own lovely company. I look around; I hear the sounds of shoes on the floor. I smile. Because I like it; I love smiling. It is as simple as that. I will smile for myself. I forget about fashion and give myself time. I choose where to have dinner. Joy. I exhale. I want healthy environments, as life should be. To persist, on this day of beauty and lightness, I want to hear music. Imagine it achieving its fullness, bending buildings with attitude — music and me.

This Sunday, I will learn with cognition to savor the colors, to understand the tones and to share everything — the gentleness of waiting, of thanking, of looking and smiling, without demands, with hope. This is how I want to be.

•••

**feelings
truths
choices**

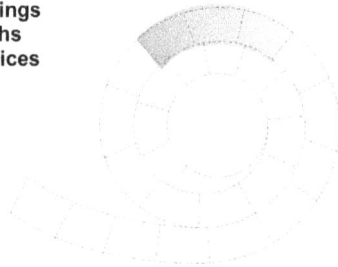

a place in the family

While your worst enemy is your own ignorance, forget about the external difficulties. Go wash your face and look in the mirror, a shocking conflict, but it is wonderful for the transformation of the dream into something real to be lived.

Personality

Every initiative of a change makes sense only if there is a very clear purpose. Questioning just for the sake of questioning, changing just for the sake of changing is the more efficient way to exhaust your strength, your time and your life.

You are a "normal" person. Like almost everyone else, you love routines and patterns; surrendering to what you know is something so determinant that it seems to be part of human nature, and not necessarily working in our favor. Ask questions of your fears, of your suspicions. It is necessary to take advantage of fear, in a situation like this. Call all your selves to the discussion. From your brain to your guts, all will participate. It is time for honesty. Your personality is in construction. Make an effort to get from every cell of your body the certainty that the change was worth it. Eradicate the diseases before they think of taking you.

Every change must come from two certainties: That something does not fit the fate you seek and that our entire being is sure of what must be stopped, eradicated, or removed. Only then will you be whole, with your full potential integrated, seizing every chance for transformation; even if they come from tragedy or from someone else's achievement.

Creativity

I could not sleep. The night is so long when you do not have peace. I am tired of thinking. From a deeper level of consciousness, I hear a "shut up." It is my disconfirming and subjugated side, the side that has been indoctrinated, went to school and has a doctorate degree that asks me for silence. Why worry so much about other people's concept of reality?

I feel overwhelmed. I have always had my opinions. I seek knowledge. I need to understand things. And sometimes I see I have been acting aloof. Everything has been seen — what has been; what is; and what will be. And I am here, in disbelief.

How is it possible? Did Dragons really once exist? Did Cyclopes? In the animated movies, the avatars control air and fire; they are masters of the elements. In contemporary India, they are healers, wise men. Even children know that. They see facts intuitively, such as the existence of fish in the sea or plants in the forests. They accept the knowledge the world offers them with a perfect notion of logic, without the demanding of evidence. They do not know that they know; they are not so arrogant. They learn what is taught to them. They respect their own timing. How does one imagine, after all, a forest without plants? How does one doubt the fish in the sea, a past without wisdom or life? What is this labyrinth, where does childhood get entangled, as it creates its leaves through friction?

They grow up in an environment sometimes impossibly wide. There are adults who doubt that dinosaurs existed. Even after seeing the fossils in museums. And they also doubt interplanetary journeys, even with so much recorded video. They doubt the evolution of life, the repeated rebirth of continents, glaciers, extinct plants and animals, of consciousness. How do you wake up? It is necessary to have peace, to sleep in the first place; to hear the shouts — cries of children who want to grow up, to become adults — and to be awake. Now. Right now.

It is extraordinary to watch the formation of a generation with so many perspectives, a knowledge that does not make them different, but contemporary — avid, modern, open to new possibilities. They see themselves in the mirror. Their doubts are confessable. They develop musculature and vocabulary. They are seeds of life, justified in a moment, a work, a gesture. And that demands celebration.

What about their wishes? On what ground do their minds walk? Where should the hands that support them be? What do they seek? They have beans and potatoes for dinner. What are they thirsty for? What should be served at the table? Memories, values, speaking or listening; a voice, a world, a mother… Everything. The good and the bad, accepted as a whole. To see a unity in them, a perennial contrast. And through them, manifest the instruments to search for balance. To achieve it is our reason for being — eternal, modern and timely.

Knowledge: That is what the "question" is about — limited and concrete. Imagination encompasses the whole world — the quest — the reason. I search for stability and abundance. Riches, nature, agony — in a universe tending to equilibrium, the elements simply dislocate. Me? I just want to get up, walk in the world, to be a part of it — easy to satisfy — abundant in my ignorance; forget about all the rest and stabilize my world.

•••

movement
reality
objective

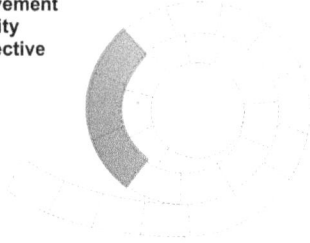

image

This inner disposition to hear oneself brings new elements to the conversation; the child and the elderly; experience and the fear — but mainly courage. It takes you faster to your happiness, and reduces unnecessary waste and stress.

Education

Every champion needs courage to realize what their ideals bring. Their values; properly acknowledged and organized to mean something, must be compensated; in the soul and in the pocket.

As a counterpoint, all inadequate practices must be punished with irrevocable abandonment. There is always some gain when one cultivates resilience and extirpates weakness, inertia and conformism. Coherence in what one does is very important.

Learn how to interact, dressed as courage, as a child, as a parent, as a human. As a kid, everything that is necessary is there, in your memories; in words heard and attitudes misunderstood; in facts repeated. Imagine a pencil and many sheets of paper. Allow yourself to bring to the surface the widest array of values, reasons and objections of your family members. The more you access your memory, the more information will be made available to

you.

The more you accept the suggestions you receive, the more ideas you will have. If you are brave, you will look for the best ones and practice them, whatever the source may be.

Limits

That a scare. What is this noise? It comes from the kitchen. It is the children. They have grown; they have learned what a Sunday is. They let us sleep. They take a shower and sit at the table. They have clean hands. They even choose their clothes to wear. They have personality; they match the colors to their mood. They set their own nature free.

What about their ideas? How is this possible, their subjects, their arguments? When did I start to argue? When I got my second job? Maybe I am not the best judge. Maybe I was obedient for too long, but I do not remember arguing with my parents or my teachers. These are memories of an apprentice — my memories. I have always been thirsty for learning, for knowing, for changing. To argue, one needs to know the facts, to have knowledge to express. Especially, when one is against something.

These mornings, I question their education; whether

to discipline, the ideas or the tenor of discussion? Is forbiddance the solution? Who likes disagreements? How to alter a path, if the discussion is allowed, but the action is forbidden?

It is necessary to have emotional intelligence, to feel; to swallow; to digest; and possess good communication skills to give clear answers; and even more, specific knowledge about what one says in a fraction of a second. The children have this — they live in a world where grades and stages seem to have disappeared. They plant forests in their dreams, and nurture them frequently with details and facts — from there, without thorns, transformation blossoms. And I know there is some sadness in their view of the world; in their way of relating to people; in the reality they begin to live.

For the sake of setting limits, we exhaust our energy to discipline our kids; we put them in boxes, literally, where a corner is a corner and a side is a side. This is how it works, and I did not see it, did not realize it. If something is missing, they look for it, they go beyond boundaries. They show an innate capacity to love without end. And because they have no set direction, they take the ones which are proximate — the mother; the father; the guitar.

We were like that, but now, as adults, we have become too artificial to notice. We do not see the quest. To these sounds of childhood, which move to a new school year, the practices of sports, has now added learning to silence the sounds of steps, stealth — walking and becoming silent. What kind of baggage will they carry? It makes me remember, almost makes me feel the weight of days. And then it is done. The history is written. Only nostalgia can wake us up, as a flash of light, reminding us of how it used to be — perhaps of how it will be someday.

Sometimes, the big one runs away from the little ones' box; someone like Pablo Picasso comes and reaches the intrinsic highness of creation, integrating lines, eyes, noses and curves in unexpected contours, showing us that there are other views of what we call real. There are other windows on reality, new perspectives of things we think belong to us. A myth is born — one that does not hide any secrets, but lets them be seen by those who want to discover them. With their skill, a skill that comes so easy for them, children convince us of the beauty that already exists; as they look at straight lines, as a protest, they see curves.

I wonder if artists, as children, had their notion of

limits neglected. Did they walk along other landscapes? At what age did they start to argue; to make calculations; to express their knowledge; to acquire knowledge from apple trees, like Isaac Newton, or from lightning, like Benjamin Franklin; to let curiosity jump over the wall to watch the clouds go by?

Every baby is a creative theorist, to some extent. Their minds stimulate investigation, and at the same time they research, they make their ideas concrete. They throw away possibilities and absorb affirmations. Scientist who cannot speak yet. Not finding certainties pre-existing on shelves, feeding the imagination and the capacity to generate alternate paths, is patently important. At what point are they taken seriously? Did they have mirrors?

Every childhood might be recalcitrant. Children grow up, and disturb what is already settled; they pick flowers, topple bookcases, mix up certainties; they confuse tact and authenticity, gentleness and truth; they throw to the wind the whole discourse on values, respect, trust; they embarrass society; simply, they are direct. If we do not like what they offer, are we obliged to accept? And what if it is at grandma's Sunday dinner?

•••

iniciative
evolution
education

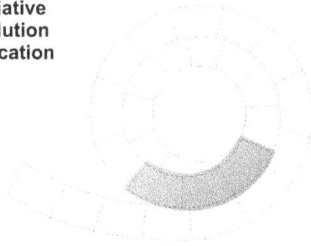

beliefs

Living cannot be delegated — except to those who are ultimately responsible for moving their own legs and taking the next step. Doing is something concrete, specific. Rethink your education. Recover your values. This is your starting point on the way to victory.

Attitude

During the training of a champion, you were taught, since the beginning, to perceive the environment around you — places, people, teaching; and from this arsenal, to select your weapons to reach success. Now, a new stage begins, where you become the player in training. The baggage you have accumulated has already changed you. The necessary raw materials have been internalized. This is the moment to focus attention on the inside, and get ready to take the hold of your own destiny.

Your next challenge is to go beyond your convictions. It is always easier to surround yourself only with ideas, situations and people you like. It is also simpler to take the more travelled way, the experience that worked — to like and to have done are not enough, however. There is much more to come.

Intelligence and energy seem to come with birth, but various skills are acquired on your mother's lap; from your grandmother's tales; in fights among siblings; and with time, at school and at work, where your knowledge is tested. You have been trained to take command of chaos, and at the right moment turn decision into action — rising above your own resistance to untried methods. It does not matter what will come out of it. Time is your ally, and the process only ends when your will to win — which works on your side as long as you have it — decides to retire, dismissing you from the foray.

Your nature was firmly rooted in its coexistence with family. There, the notions of kindness and gratitude were imprinted on your character — from the perception that you are able to serve; to do; to achieve your self-confidence. From the recognition of what has been given, a burning, latent energy is born; a brave predisposition that is ready to overflow into action.

Accessing your self-confidence and with a lot of encouragement, you are the master of your fate. Through your actions, words and thoughts, you become the conductor of the facts.

Effervescence

Hey. Pssst. Are you awake? Open the door, arise from your dreams. Let us talk. I want to talk about games, about the television episode I watched yesterday, about my thoughts, about the ideas I keep having. Can you hear the breeze? It rocks the house gently, and blows the mind when it haunts me, taking away my calm.

I lose myself in words that echo everywhere, among the actions which demand much of me when I feel paralyzed; when mobility hunts me and shakes me. I do not want to hear. I want to talk, to play, to laugh; and a new life, full of perfume. I think a lot about how things are and how they can be — about what I can do and what they want me to do. I need to decide. But I am still so small. Why should it be easy?

Who believes in me? Who needs to believe? Who do I need to believe me? They imagine and wait for something; but as they work, argue, sleep they do not see my suffering. I am not an object; I rebel, I want to transcend. I will drink some water. More water.

I need ways to make these locked up ideas flow; for some are already hardening — and only make sense in new pastures, new lands. I need to discover them, to transcend this state. We are all dominated by a state of spirit, like a tyrant that governs us. And the result is that most of us cannot see anymore.

Hey, wake up. You are always disturbing me. Can you not see I need to teach you? To sweep away this perception, this consensus, to explode step by step to wake you up. But I promise that in this war of consciousness, I will be your ally. I can see flowers, even in the mud. We can preserve them.

Today is Sunday. It is time. There is not much time. Let us meet for dinner. There is so much to do. I already do so much every day, but do I do what is necessary? It is in "this game of life" that I do what is needed of me. Like men, the adults, those who determine the economy and the currency exchange, those who kill the brilliance. I am what I do. My arms no longer stretch. But I like what I wear. Do they not see that what I am and do are part of me?

Sometimes I only do it because I know they want it that way — like today when life seems to be a game there is something beyond the rules that define the facts, the strategies. It is, only in allowing yourself to become intrigued; involved in these discussions; arguing with the others — that you will convince yourself of these truths. I have brains that pulse, grow, call me. Do you hear?

Come on, wake up. Even if the day is over, the fight goes on. I want to talk. For me, for my sadness — my hope; to make the future flow, I need you. Hear me. I know that new ideas generate counter reactions.

Sometimes they make history; they change the views of the world; at other times, they provoke secret fears, and because of this they are torn apart and discarded. Believe. Save this impulse. Help me, use reason and make ideas concrete. Come with me, now.

It is almost time; in a few moments we will have dinner. It will be the future. Where are we going today? I love to go. When I get there, I am perceived.

•••

consciousness
certainties
transformation

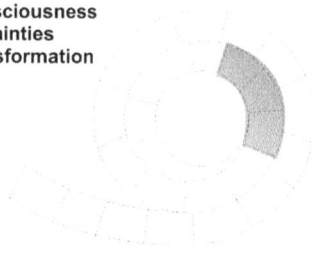

roots

Attitude comes from truth — from an authentic coexistence with the soul. Nobody is able to make difficult decisions; to take unpopular positions and keep loyal to their beliefs, if they do not know who they are and feel comfortable that way.

It is necessary to know yourself, to face the real world; to walk with the steps of those who are masters of their fate — genuine conquerors, lords of authenticity.

Certain positions you take in your life can change your heart. Even more than the environment, the power of your words takes you from an endless celebration of past deeds to a deep inspiration that encourages new action.

Before you become the leader of your own destiny, your success has been limited to survival. At this moment, such leadership means an ascension to new heights; the realization of dreams that you have set as goals; and the strengthening of your courage to act — all dependent on your capacity to control fear, to be self-confident at the right moment, to take appropriate action and to always fight against the gravity of negativism.

Maturity

The marks of our relationship with other people are not erased. After all, what is eternity made of? It is made of memories, of what you have felt and have made felt. Only where there is life is there feeling.

Besides being abstract, feelings are abundant. They are different in shape, in tone, in dose, in effect. They go beyond what we judge as necessary. Sometimes, they deteriorate, fade away; are lost due to negligence. They do not leave roots. Remember, champion, focus. You need to evaluate if the right feelings are associated with the right actions.

You are still in training. You know that you need to train and be trained. And every member of this team called family must keep guiding and criticizing, to help you improve your performance in all aspects. Your trainers promise to awaken skills that, in the right way and at the right moment, will be of use to the world. Anger and fear, patience and dedication, all deserve to triumph.

The main tactics are to face all relationships with honesty and action. Argue, yes, but about the subjects that can be negotiated — nothing more — fight, but for peace. This is the secret of success.

Mistakes

It is already morning. I need to face the day; the sun is high in the sky. I need to get up from this bed and live. I do not like this life, this house; these obligations. This is not what I have always dreamed of. I have trained so hard. I have done so many push-ups. I have bought so many clothes. I have chosen my friends; have not yielded to my desires; and what for? Without noticing, while I did what had to be done, life went by, the years passed. People have disappointed me, and that hurts, hurts deeply — a nameless pain which the mind drags here and there but cannot erase.

I do not want to go back, to live everything again. It is too much trouble. It is impossible to repeat everything; in a hurry to act, but thinking slowly. I feel like setting fire to myself; to burn and to be reborn from the ashes. I would never let anyone disappoint me; I would spend less;

obey some people more and other people less; try harder; ignore and err.

Among us common people, the unknown is a synonym for wrong. This is what science is made for, starting from an error to build something new; increasing knowledge, from mistake to mistake, seeking foundation and evidence. Ah, I would definitely err more often. Study more. Eliminate less. My hands would not be dirty. What about this oddment fear — the shame, the opinions of others? Who invented these curses? I would take them all and throw them into a hope chest, which I would seal with a lock and hide underground, in a hole as deep as the one where I was thrown my whole life.

What do I do now with what they think of me? Using it or repressing it, the feeling of despite is the same. And where do I put the shame that paralyzed me? And the fear that shortened my paths, limited my actions, made my days exactly the same?

My head hurts. Why to live? Why to fight? To beat the fear, the shame, the opinions which will never be mine? None of this keeps me company. Fear has already achieved its purpose. Nothing happens, everything is always the same. Opinions are gone, with the people who mattered to me.

There is only shame left, shame of what I let happen. I see in the mirror the remorse for what I have not been, and deeply miss the person I did not let myself be. It is shame that forces me to get up day after day; that makes me take a shower, get dressed, go to work and pretend I am happy, so I will not feel even more embarrassed. It is shame that encourages me to smile and play when I feel like crying and screaming — which I never let myself do.

Shame has nurtured me. It has put on display only the best there is. It has made me ready to live with those who like me and those who I dislike. It has saved me in the jungle. It has taught me diplomacy; the critical subjects and gestures that almost always work — sympathy and cheerfulness the reactions that keep me integrated in the society that surrounds me and controls me. I get dressed with it. I eat with it, satisfying a hunger that devours itself. Without desires, only complying; I had temper tantrums; I fell asleep and I woke up with it. It never sleeps, however.

Now I understand. One of the strongest reasons why men are attracted to art and science is the desire to escape their daily experiences. The accumulation of goods, of knowledge, of events becomes the focus of their emotional life. They seek the safety and the peace that can only be achieved if they follow the requisite wind toward their fate. I did not know what mine was.

When dinnertime came, I wore my sadness and, with a painted smile, buttoned up my suffering. I got ready to chew on situations and swallow my pain, smiling and bleeding inside. Deep, very deep inside, I have been happy. I have dreamed, I have believed. Where did I stop, without even noticing? The others have also dreamed, as someone who has not lived. Do all those smiles taste like tears? Have they really saved themselves from pain? Can they teach me? Is there time to learn, to shed the skin and carry the world like a breeze, to flow, to win, and to dream again? Who is coming with me?

I do not want to be old anymore; to grow old and dry up; to lose water, the flow, the movement. It is very sad, but sometimes it happens during childhood. To delay old age, however, is wonderful; leave it for tomorrow, for the day after tomorrow. In a glimpse, I see that the divine subtlety is to leave time to our hands. And my time is now.

To survive, I need to face the shocks. They are all necessary. The important thing is the choice that comes later, what to rebuild. To be open is crucial. Even nature rewards species that adapt to changes, with alterations that are visible in physical appearance — as your own heritage, is revitalized and purified.

Now, I have learned how to learn; how to eat better. I absorb the looks and I hear between the lines. At dinner, I want more than spaghetti and salad — I look for a path. We have lived in families since the beginning of time. Will we never understand one another? I want your spark, your wisdom. I want to hear you, to see you. Today, I want you.

•••

power
foundation
lessons

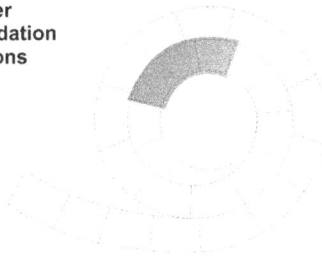

cohabitation

The world of those who look you in the eye and let their hair down has many crossroads. It is important to know how to go back and not feel guilty, remember that it is up to you to detect the mistakes and rectify them.

Whoever takes measures to bring reason and emotion back into the game, lives fully with dignity and respect for themselves and for Mankind; and learns how to replace the values and attitudes in the short-circuit, whose spark hinders their balance. With this they grow and transmit a message to every single cell in their bodies that no feeling is greater than the one who carries it.

Life

The time has come. Define your position right at the start of the next encounter, and emphasize frequently where you want to go. You are completing your reformation.

Start assuming that the difficulties are bigger than they seem. Do not waste your time denying the cycle or its obstacles. Next, assume the mental posture of one who believes that there are no secrets in the world; that everyone will end up finding out everything, knowing all of the strategies.

Expect your play to be received in the worst possible way, generating unpredicted results. Now you know that it is your destiny to win. You can do it.

With an increase in activity, some muscles might hurt, some cells might rebel and develop diseases; the eyes might get tired from so much crying, but doing something is necessary. The sleeves are rolled up; it is time to live.

Wind

I will open the windows; turn on the music; make some coffee; and I will go for a walk; meet the wind; feel the breeze on my face; let the sun burn me; the rain soak me; let the sweat roll down my body. I will explode with the energy that fills me; tell the world that I am not here on holiday; say good morning; and if the answer is cold, I will look at the sun and look for my way; my good morning.

Today I will not work. No urgent reports, no people anesthetized by the rush of material survival. No dinners with the right people, no politically correct menus; the whole day from coffee to coffee.

I will take a deep breath; feel my heart speed up; exercise my hands; look the doorman in the eyes when he gives me the newspaper; and say, "thank you;" I will see the hole in the pavement and walk around it; I will look for an ordinary place, one that I pass by every day, and find it beautiful.

I do not fool myself. I prefer the frantic routine pushing me, making me produce as if I was a piece in a machine, or a raindrop falling from the roof; being part of a whole, believing that my part makes a difference — but for whom?

The answer is wet; like the rain that irritates those who do not like life. It is all mud, dreamless; or those who do not have time and simply move forward, numb and insipid, living a life of nightmares. I confess that sometimes I too get irritated with the rain. No one needs to know my shortcomings, my resentments.

It was in that rain that I found myself. Getting all wet, I heard the sound of life. I understood that the rain causes irritation because it is alive, and I did not know how to live. If everyone could watch themselves from a distance, they would notice the breadth of their lives; take them more seriously, right and wrong; good and bad. Something is good or bad according to its effect upon each one of us. The rest is only passing clouds.

Now I am no longer like that. I choose to learn in every aspect. If intuition is perception, the mind needs to attend. Look at the rain. Open a space for the image. Follow the raindrops. And accept the message. It does not matter if takes a second or an entire century. The important thing is to make proliferation possible, make it perpetual, in the memory and in the attitude —with a lot of oxygen.

I will order my brain to produce more adrenaline. And race towards my destiny, under the light that has illuminated me since I was born. I will reach the point where others have not been. In this way, it is good to start observing what other people have not, as I encounter the breeze, keeping a dialogue with the wind; I will listen beyond the words, hear the answer that smells like grass, and act. God, how good this is.

I acknowledge my power. I allow myself to think. I let myself enjoy, dream. I stretch my arms, throw my head back and look up. I widen my perspectives. I prolong my life while I stretch my legs, one and then the other. Step by step. I am tired.

I will say goodbye to the wind, slowly, with immense pleasure. Walk slowly and firmly, full of endorphins, lactic acid, heat and sweat. I will walk around the holes, close to the sewers, a way that I know now. I will teach myself to see the grass, that it was invisible for me yesterday and now is a fact. With the same eyes, I will read the newspapers.

Train my mind to think; thinking — one of the best values of education. I drink more coffee, take a shower and get dressed for dinner. I turn off the music and close the windows, without closing off my soul and turning off life.

This state of consciousness sounds like the truth. Pure, without anguish, the rain washed away all the hurt. There are now only the reports, which I write like those who make a wish — I try to make them better and better. From business meetings, I absorb every detail; and I feel that it is the spice that will offer me the dinners I choose. I drink my coffee, drop by drop, and command my brain: "Use yourself". I hear the doorbell as I capture everything around me. I open the package. I codify. I produce more and better.

Now, I can drink more water, beer and wine. And then, with the dignity of a contemporary citizen, savor my Sunday, feeling the satisfaction sliding down my neck, hungry for life; the pleasure of being, doing, making it happen. And at the end of the day, say thanks to life for waking me up, making me aware of a different Sunday.

May the day be good and grand throughout dinner; throughout a pleasant walk; in the tranquility of bills paid; in the savings for future Sundays; may those be frequent and have a route and a rhythm, like light — different, full of crossroads; with the smell of lavender of those who have just arrived.

•••

celebrate

Every reform requires work, causes pain, but it is fundamental. It demands concrete solutions and a full reformulation of the ways of seeing, analyzing and acting. After it begins, nothing will be like before; frequently changing careers and lives; it almost never ends without some blood on the floor and a human being standing, now even stronger.

To be free and feel a sense of achievement, you must have integrity and intelligence. It is certain that you will survive. However, only with maturity will you be able to respect the emotions of others, abandon your arrogance and finally fly.

To be like the ones who seem to have been born ready. They do not know what will come, but are sure of what to do. They seem to have something, an innate talent for determining what is important — a category of player that feed on water, flow across the world and conquers what they want to, without taking notice that sometimes wanting is all is required.

Always

Celebrate. Hear the song, or sing it. Appreciate the arts. Cheer with the sports. Overcome the material and discover new landscapes.

Enjoy the end of the battle, the beginning of love, the money in the bank, the handshake. The masters of their own fate celebrate with a passion.

Their joy is sincere, deep and genuine. Their ability of advancing, of prospering in their actions, deserves applause. Now, you have consistence. And the necessary courage to make difficult and radical decisions, like saying yes or no.   It is time to savor the results.

Stop. Listen. Transcend.

Accept the invitation and get closer to God.

All Power and Glory to the Lord

I like praying. If the world is energy, this is the synchrony I choose. I appreciate the grandiosity of the prayer, the magnitude of this power, of being able to talk to and be heard by the Almighty. It makes me feel good, to be an instrument of a greater work. I feel useful making a difference; being different; walking hand in hand with the difference.

I find time for everything, and it is time to go to the home of the Divine. I go in the morning; I start my day illuminated. I have everything. My life is good. I have problems, but the problems do not have me. Nothing is bigger than this power that emanates from life and love. I have much to be grateful for. And as long as I live, I want to be connected to what is best. I want positive energy, health, ideas, dreams, plans, faith.

He who has God has everything. I want His will to impregnate all my being and guide every step I take; teach me to talk at the right time; to use the right words; to be silent; to listen. Give me intelligence to study and wisdom to act.

"Oh, Father, be always the shield that protects me and the light that guides me. I will get ready, inside and out. It does not matter how my best is worse than others. God knows us; He knows what we have to give; and what we need to receive and overcome. May His wonders be manifested in my life."

I always leave renovated after a meeting with God; ideas and desires are stronger than ever. Deep inside, regardless of religion, I believe that God's will is that we leave His house full of life, never doubting about the realization of dreams; believing in them; setting goals and dates; ready, intellectually, emotionally and financially, for the next step; to make it happen.

And if someone asks me why I connect with God, I will tell the truth, "to be happy; to say thanks." I will hear, sing, pray; and when I come back, we will all have dinner, together.

•••

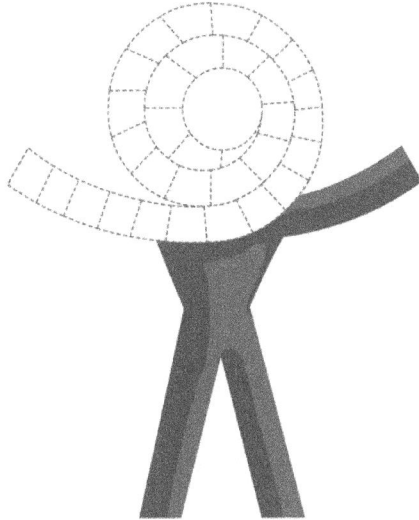

I could add that to dedicate some time to listen, be honest with and respect yourself, in a kind of internal dynamism and introversion, generally makes you feel better. But the results speak for themselves, loud and clear. Life hears them, and casts them into eternity.

Part III

Configuration of the Game

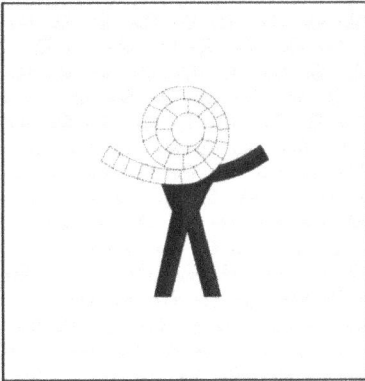

SUNDAY - THE GAME

Participants: _____

Results: _____

Washing the hands: _____
Entree: _____
Main Course: _____
Dessert: _____
Coffee: _____
Liquer: _____

The board

The virtual board is a Sunday. To configure it, the player will determine:

- The awakening: the stage of life he is in;
- The participants: what will be the strategy they use;
- The dinner itself: what the desired result is;
- The following Sundays.

Everything starts when your eyes open; you become aware it is Sunday — a day culturally dedicated to leisure that takes you away from the whirlwind of daily routine. Since there is no work on Sundays, children do not go to school. On Sundays, families meet.

Guided by events that this gathering generates, right or wrong follows, continuing until the day when you, the player, decide to reconfigure your image. This can be done at any moment during this game; and as a consequence it will alter the desired results and the strategies used.

If you prefer, the configuration of the family might be static, speechless and without action; it might be without space for expressing itself, either by words or behavior; or it might also be passive, listening — suffering the actions and reacting as you chose.

If you choose to be part of an "active family", with different age ranges, you will have the possibility of including them in any stage of the game.

It is important to highlight that in a "static" or "passive" family configuration, you take control of the board, but not of the results. Other elements may interfere with the match. The game has its tricks to force the application of the lessons learned during the training of the champion. Our player knows every single one, and must pay attention to identify them in order to win.

On the other hand, in the "active family" configuration, every move is performed, every choice is made by all the players — how to wake up; where to have dinner; their place. The combination of these options will form a scenario. So, no player will have control over the board's context, and no option will be irrelevant.

The crucial difference between the players will once again be the champion's training. You, the "star player", are the only one to have it, and this places you in the position of the favorite.

You use your own judgment when confronted with the choices of other players. After all, freedom must be exercised and respected by everyone. Everything converges upon a single event — dinner.

Every Sunday has its own character, many countenances — coziness; despair, like autumn; the tranquility of those who have chosen the best of dreams. It is not written on their faces how much money they have earned. You have to digest as therapy, with pleasure, or antacid, the other characters or players but, essentially yourself — the one that wakes up every Sunday in a different state of mind. The appetite you feel for the things of life is not always the same, nor is your hunger.

During the game, the results will be determined by the answers given by each participant. To alter the positions on the board, you need to wait for the next Sunday. As one Sunday follows another, each match allows for a new configuration of the board. Everything can be included or excluded — events; contacts with unknown energies; your own movements and the movements of others.

But it is necessary to survive until then. Routine waits at the door, holding a bag, brushing your coat. Your family has left you with scars; reinforced, deep, obfuscated. You cannot remove them, pack them up and hide them away in a closet. From dinner, you bring a kiss, a slap, spaghetti breath. You want more kisses. You do not deserve the slap. You love spaghetti.

Shall we have dinner?

You, your character, have already adopted an image — you have a given age; you know what you want from life; you know whether the storms you face bring lightning, or bosses, financial problems or weakened health.

You know what makes you afraid and what makes you stronger. You have discovered where the light is, the path to follow amidst tempests, but with very clear objectives.

This path always starts at home, when you wake up. It is important to visualize your address; the type of housing; the daily living environment; the interests that fill this world. These are the landmarks of what is familiar, and there are so many, or so few, to perceive that sometimes you get confused and they all look the same, as grains of sand. However, you do not wander around. You know what's important. You face strong winds; and when you feel tired, you go back to your own world — your home, your belongings, your scars, your pain.

It is necessary to illuminate every corner of the house, to identify the shadows and reshape your world, to bring it closer to your objectives. In the elements of your private world, you recognize the people in your family. The journey of our lives draws, sculpts, writes and shapes our history. You are hungry for life.

The days go by — rainy, sunny, cold, warm, cloudy. One Sunday follows another. Moods change; the family is present in smells, flavors, nutrients for the body, the soul, the mind. Remembering old disagreements is inevitable, before the digestion does its job and changes every food particle into a seed of knowledge. Those are bright, frustrated looks. You smile, scream, fight, love. Enjoy everything and everyone.

Sunday after Sunday, your character is repeated. As in a spiral, one cycle follows the other in a search for values. You appreciate what you expect, what you have, what you have been, what you hope to be someday. Only you know what your character really loves, how strong this love is and what you are willing to do to get it. The shadows are overcome by light and the spiral becomes tighter; the structure reveals the paths travelled by it.

There are days when you wake up as a child and go

to sleep tired, and despite it all, you go on waking up and going to sleep, with effort, tired. You keep walking through streets and thoughts. You live in a home that is so familiar; you do not even notice it anymore. You keep feeding yourself; sometimes with jabuticaba, other times with faith. Step by step, you write your history in your own world, your own dream, your own territory.

Much more than simply following conventions, rules and duties, you have a role to play in the family of your universe. You choose your place, without even noticing, and your acts are etched in it. At the same time, you satisfy your own needs, you assume the weight of your own being. You create a fact; choose a possibility and throw away the rest, while digesting and savoring.

This is the share of existence that is yours. You have to act or let yourself be guided. Does it always work like this? Are all Sundays hot, rainy or cloudy? Could all words be crucial treaties?

Everybody is hardly the same. Change is necessary; taking a walk is possible. Go to the Father, look at the Mother; take your eyes away from the plate full of beans and look at your hands, examining whatever the moment brings with a magnifying glass. Observe what is done; what is said; what is served — at times miserably critical, other times deeply solicitous.

Adopt the perspective of those who are ready; abandon the ordinary; have dinner with an appetite.

The table is laid. The menu and the tablecloth are transitory. Which is relevant are the moment, and your personal approach. Everything is in your hands — enjoying, savoring, celebrating or despising; letting the moment grow cold, until it freezes, till you no longer hear it, or your child, your soul, the radio, inanimate influences.

Chewing, talking with gestures, words and eyes; or who knows, imagining that you are far away or closer; that you have much more or much less; conscious enough to remember God and get things off your chest, deeply and silently; sharing the salad; holding on to the inevitable and accepting what you really are. You believe, and your beliefs support you — a dessert for the spirit, occupying empty spaces, filling voids and leaving a sweet taste in the mouth.

You are sitting in your chair, trying to get comfortable. You accidently drop a fork; bending down to pick it up, you discover other feet under the table. Feet like yours. You notice other types of shoes, other forms of leaving. You are surprised that they are so different and yet so close, how did it take so long for you to see it?

With your arms, you push the chair back, but the disturbing noise comes from your feet. You go to the cupboard and open a drawer. Your fingers look for another fork; the old excuse no longer works, and you need to use a new one. You comb your hair with your fingers, close the drawer and go back to your dear ones, occupying your place — which strangely does not seem the same.

Now, you notice your own clothes. How long have you dressed like that? Some pieces of clothing we wear become part of our lives, as if they were extensions of our bodies, a complement to our personalities. On Sunday, especially, it is difficult to determine what you have chosen, the outfit or a character who wears it. You do not think; you act. You allow the finished part of your personality to extend outside the body, and simply show itself, be what it is.

After all, there is no work on Sundays. There is time and space to take care of you, quench the thirst of the body, the soul, the mind. It does not matter how much you love, approve or hide; deep inside of you, there is a curiosity that moves you and an impulse that propels you; your most heartfelt proclivities. On Sundays, everything can be manifested without defenses; choosing faith, the water, the world.

Your shoes follow you everywhere; to the hammock, the shade, the table. So many steps. You have your style of walking — slow, firm, shuffling; without censorship. After all, what is a Sunday? It is time on your hands; dinner on the table, in the kitchen, at the bar, at your mother's house.

How many people come to dinner walking in their Sunday shoes, with an open heart? Where do they go, how do they enjoy a Sunday? How many people do you want to share your Sunday with?

Those, the chosen ones, belong to your "heart family"; you go to the Sunday game together; you walk in the street; run in the park; kneel to pray; throw out the garbage, pick a table and share the food. The members of the family are hungry players who get together to satisfy that hunger, and then go back to their destinies.

The menu does not change; it is the moment when everyone gathers at the table; looking, talking, hearing, then playing their different roles; afterwards disagreeing about the world, on the sofa, in the kitchen, on the road. Nobody lives another's life. More than the hug, a step is necessary. Everybody needs to move forward. If this step is not taken a void will remain and the world will never know what could have been.

What goes on in your mind? Your thoughts follow you in the street, get into the car, go on the bus with you; they are your guides; your clothes, your mood, your teeth. In some countries, you can tell the school someone attended just hearing their accent. Many communities can tell the general health condition of a person looking at their teeth.

Society knows, from the clothes someone wears, where they have been. How is your health? What do you talk about? How do you express your sense of humor? What is your school? Where do you go during the week? How is your spirit today? What do you do on Sundays?

On Sundays, you make choices. And frequently they are the same — the same table, the same choice of food, the same laughter, the same feelings, and who knows how many times the same dream. In your words, you carry the community that surrounds you, the house that welcomes you, the life that teaches you. You walk, talk, eat, you silence yourself. You are hungry.

The smells are magic; potions that wake you up and make you fall asleep. You are not always awake enough to notice them, in the body, in places, in sounds. Waking up is diving into the world. It is necessary to touch, to hear, to feel the scents; and to remember the joys of the past, the skin you have touched, the hardships you have faced. Life can be recurrent, sometimes scentless, taking you through childhood, youth, maturity — and back again.

Some options are in fact indigestible, and cannot always be avoided; but when known about them, they can be prevented and fixed. Sunday, wherever you are, is a day to be and to savor; wine, bacon, sweets; kisses, screams, ardor; the table, the dishes, the cereal. To see, to smell, to do and to say thanks — everything you need to be what you want to be is what life offers you during this dinner.

Every master of every subject you have not yet studied is at the table. You need eyes to see them. You want to learn how to network, to influence, to determine north and to decide a heading; to determine how good it is to know, to recognize your favorite flavor, the desired goal. And then move toward it.

To hear the sound of a voice, of a song, of a scream — to find the right tone. What time is it? Who is there? A human being with a body, with ideas, with a state of mind, and your family, with its smells, talks, pains, loves. They share the hunger and satisfy themselves with life. During this meal, the reformation is finished. It is time to spin.

The player you have created, that this book has trained, is ready to shine, to illuminate the others, the facts — to arrive to new conclusions and feel new sensations, extending the possibilities of altering your situation; to bless your training, the effort of your trainers, the sweat on your face; to be yourself, and much more than a winner, a trainer.

Next Sunday, you will widen your views, initiate actions, promote peace and positive action — for yourself, first and foremost, and then, by consequence, for others. They await you at the table. Shall we have dinner?

Topics for Players

In this game, and in life, it is not enough to own the ball, to be responsible for the configuration of the board. Different forces cross our path, allowing us to see other landscapes. Circumstances are beyond our control. When facing the new, the vast knowledge we have acquired seems insufficient. The game, as life, has its strategies and its results. And your next challenge is:

- Topics for beginners: People
- Topics for intermediate players: Facts
- Topics for advanced players: Ideas

As a player, you are not limited to a single profile. The important thing is to try and answer each challenge, quickly, naturally and sincerely.

With every stage of the dinner, questions will be made about people, facts and ideas. Be brave. Identify the people, go straight to the facts and renew your ideas.

Part IV

The Game

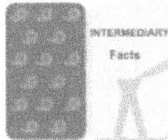
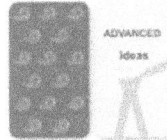

Washing your Hands

Coexisting with the differences

Everyone is coming today. May there be peace. I have cleaned the house, organized the living room, and washed the bathrooms. Everything smells like hope. The table is laid. I have set the cutlery and combed my hair. In the kitchen, everything is ready. The dishes are washed. There are no signs of the fight. I woke up early and worked quickly, and now I can smile.

I will hug them when they arrive, and secretly wish that God guides them all. I will kiss them, ask them the right questions. Some do not like to be kissed. They have not had the time to discover that a kiss is a delicate gesture, the subtlety of love. I like watching the dance of the lipstick, which leaves lips and colors faces. Some come to dinner already thinking of leaving. Some others, who prefer a hug, will stay until late.

I will do my share of the work; serve a hot meal to everyone, and propose a toast. To touch glasses and look people in the eyes, raising my hands to celebrate. I will not allow joy to be made banal. The table is laid, life is a matter of will, and there is always hope of survival. I will thank God for His presence and prepare His place of honor. I will open the door when the bell rings and see, in their eyes, their free hearts.

Let us talk about the soap opera, about the magazine, but not about the boss. Some will arrive numb; others with their throats constricted — for those, I give the impetus of peace. I will allow them to search the drawers and alleviate the heart. I give this to myself. I spread perfume and joy. I clean the relationship and let it shine. It is better to wash your hands now.

Use water, a lot of water. Wash, clean everything that does not belong to you — dust, stains, the smeared makeup; everything that flows from the past, so that the present might find some space and take its place. Build the crystals of your dreams in the water, and let them shine. Sing, in your mind, the music of your future. Jazz or rock?

You choose the tone. Hear the sound that comes from the soul and embraces the day. Hum your wishes for the world. And let them flow.

Are there towels in the bathroom? Learn how to enjoy my hospitality. I do not want you to pass by and leave wet tracks; the newspaper left at the door suggests there is no one home. The house is quiet; gestures left in the air, already rarified. I will open the windows, two by two, to air out the room and the thoughts — to cool the space and the body.

Looking at myself in the mirror, I imagine a room full of mirrors, with special effects — they are my guests. They do not have to start with better powers to assure that they will always win, but there are details and subtleties that not everyone is able to use in their favor, like a magic magnifying glass, It is necessary to get rid of what upsets us and increase what pleases us; to invert positions to make peace, solve conflicts. Yes, blessed is the imagination, which allows us to compose scenes and simulate results.

The footsteps we leave behind and the past that we no longer live, belong to us. It is time to dry yourself of, let the world in and remembers that today is a day of light. Let the body hear the mind and, who knows, fall in love with what comes next.

Water, soap, towel; my hunger, my longing, my

mother — everything in its right place. The water has run and left a sense of longing; the soap perfumed my words and delayed my hunger — the touch of the towel brings back the mother, so beloved that sometimes I forget her. Fragments of the travelled road, reflected in my world under the same impeccable orders, rules and consequences in the universe as I understand it, with set roles to play. The same words, the same odors — always; I hate vinegar.

The window is open, and the air can circulate now — a whirlwind of souls, hungry for a place to fit in. They want to participate, to feel the skin, the pulse, the sensation of touching whoever knows the direction to go; to notice the space around you, the ground beneath your feet; to reduce to dust the discomfort that comes with emotions. Where have I left mine?

At certain moments, I feel really hungry. I hunger for rice, potatoes, space and joy; hunger for energetic people around me, people who get up in the morning and wake to life — with attitude, posture; without forgetting the luggage in the middle of the street — hungry for life; for letting footsteps on the pavement, laughter in the air and words in the memory; for seeing with a child's eyes, noticing that life jumps forward, overtakes the mind. Do you need help?

Clean hands; hungry heart; appetite for love; longing for the heat — in the body, in the themes, in the tracks. I want to be conservative and efficient, to preserve the concepts and the plates in the cupboard, discarding the cracked glasses at once; to kill the complications with practical ideas, ready for consumption; to clear misunderstandings and to act, forget, forgive; change; resume my steps, meet again the love that was forgotten, and continue on. To satisfy your hunger for life, you have to live yours fully.

•••

BEGINNERS — People | INTERMEDIARY — Facts | ADVANCED — Ideas

About people:
Who has prepared the house so you can smile?
Who hugs, kisses and looks?
Who serves, toasts and thanks the Lord?
Who speaks, setting the mood?

Who leaves tracks?

Who is reflected in the mirrors?

Who is hungry for life?

About facts:

How is the house prepared so you can smile?

What is a hug, a kiss and a look?

What is to serve, to toast and to thank the Lord?

What is spoken, setting the mood?

What are tracks?

What is reflected in the mirrors?

What is to be hungry for life

About ideas:

What does a smile say?

What to do with the hug, the kiss and the look? How to serve, to toast and to thank the Lord? How to speak, setting the mood?

What to do with the tracks?

How to deal with the images reflected in the mirrors?

How to awaken your hunger for life?

The Entrée

Expanding the observation

I know these smells; they have meant everything to me in a time when, I believe, not even time remembers anymore. Joy, safety, pleasure — today, it is herbs and fruit sauce. I take my place. I sit down. I pick up my cutlery. I serve myself time and people's presences, occupying the empty places with the moment.

I look at the table and I see people. I was lucky. I have great masters present. People who speak, chew and feel; more than the hunger of the body, they are thirsty for peace. Their ideas and behaviors have expanded my views of the world, but no longer recognize them as theirs — they have come to doubt their own power. They dismiss preliminaries and do not worry anymore — they merely show up. Where do the strong, who have planted such impetus in my soul, have their dinner?

Ah, this smell of family. Life goes on and people change. Sometimes they wilt like a flower, turn into seed and start over; other times they blossom, become large and full of branches, arguments, money in the bank and a sparkle in the eyes — everyone here, now, present at dinner, for they believe in knowledge.

Some chew with pleasure. They savor moments and foods, and get up from the table replenished. They spread across the room. You look and see their moving energy, walking, eating, speaking, and being. Others are just a promise; they blossom, get ready for what comes next, suggesting that the best is yet to come.

They look after the cutlery and the words. They choose wisely. They use whatever is available that I barely noticed it. And there are the sleepy ones, who always prefer the sofa; they lack the big appetite they should have for the long way they have walked or the nothing they have done. It does not matter if they have enjoyed themselves, a lot or almost nothing. Disbelieving, bored, they reject the appetizers. They need some pepper.

To get started, prepare, balance; you need some green — without questioning accents, dishes or spices, it is the basis of being. Try it. Be strong, hungry, and capable.

Even if it seems revolutionary to you, just go for it, with all your senses. Try new spices, and sit in different chairs; eat more slowly or quickly.

Ask your brain for other conclusions, like curious people do. To be reborn, challenge the reality of the moment; reformulate concepts and processes. Look for answers. Try new moves, visions, for sheer delight. After all, without adventure there are no new flavors, or pleasures, or discoveries.

See the salad while it is still in the garden; do not wait for it to be served at the table. To learn how to assimilate it is fundamental to observe. On the threshold of vivacity, only the greatest have the skill to make another stronger.

After all, for different appetites there are different cutlery, speeches and sensitivities. Not everyone has a good enough arsenal to discover purity disguised as ingenuity or wisdom framed as inertia; to end the wait and make the move; to act in a mischievous ambiguity that interrupts so many paths; to dismantle wars; to determine choices and conveniences; and without much pretense, makes smiles appear.

I want salt in the lettuce, in the potatoes, in the

onions which are not dishes and never will be, but make all the difference in any recipe, as a character, genuinely cheerful and communicative, that is introduced into the context and alters the general effect — not because they have some mysterious attraction, but for their simple way of magnetizing the environment, impregnating it with the smell of life, irresistible — its absence leaves a gap that can never be filled. On the other hand, its excess sickens, and does not satisfy.

Everyone wants to win. Do you have any salt?

•••

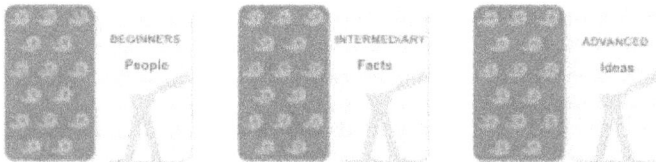

About people:

Who is strong?

Who is moving energy?

Who needs pepper?

Who is necessary?

Who precipitates smiles?

Who has salt?

About facts:

What is strength?

What is moving energy? What is pepper?

What is necessary?

What precipitates smiles?

What is salt?

About ideas:

How to be strong?

Why become moving energy? When to add pepper?

Where to be necessary? How to precipitate smiles? Would you like any salt?

The Main Course

Movements

Never despise what you have; simply want more. I get from life what I need, what I do not even know how to want. What do I want? I want to absorb from the world everything that the soul asks for; to search in the air, in a portion of rice or in love, whatever makes me brave; to penetrate a life that is yet to be lived, with no hurry, no despair; to draw the lines of the plan; to do what still needs to be done in finance, at school or in a hug.

I want to take a closer look at what is presented, and to apply it; if there is no other choice, to accept, to thank and to bless; to bear fruit. Then, I want to undo the knots in my throat and dissolve them in water; to be free to take the paths life may lead me to; to be muscle and blood, never tumor. I want to awaken new ideas, new tastes; to try some mint; to savor the encounter and to speak with joy that sometimes is not even there. I want to be bland. I want to add some olive oil. Digesting is needed.

The moment is for action; to change, to ingest the energy and assimilate it with every movement; to put the essence on the table; to exchange; to give; to find the perfect combination to survive, one that makes you stronger — everyone has their key to decode it. As for myself, I come closer to recovering mine; I search my mind for the ideals that guide me; and in my memory I keep the good wishes I receive.

In treating my needs, I save myself from starvation, as someone who recognizes life, but no longer has the eyes to see; who notices the hunger, but no longer has the strength to eat. Taste the faith. There is no time left to hesitate.

I will set my inner child loose at the table, give it space and voice, and let it enjoy the Sunday — thirsty for joy, for novelty; building neural connections, muscular fiber, emotional intelligence. How do you nurture it with the necessary hope, preparing for the journey of a life? At this stage, I know that the foundations of the world are laid.

Children of love are different. Children conceived

during intense moments, full of ecstasy, hardly ever hesitate. They are made of fibers of an unknown material which sustains them; and are naturally pushed far beyond those who are not the result of what love is.

I still do not know how far I will go, how many miles I will walk, but I see myself as a winner, and I want my inner child strong. I have a glimpse of the journey that others cannot see, and I know it is latent. I take the steps and achieve it.

Children are needy. They always want more. They look for ears and hugs; very often they are discontent, insecure. Their bones are weak. With or without pleasure, it is urgent to increase the intake of calcium and vitamin D; to learn to acquire and to overcome, but always with love.

I want to feed you with culture, education and happiness. Set your table, form your family. It is necessary to have energy and common sense to make you a human being in your universe. Never forget the truth, fried or served with sauce; that agreement is a comfort to those who measure words, a reward for the long conditioning of those who try to please their listeners. The search for flavor is commendable, but to be strong is crucial. So much agreement could choke you. I will reduce the salt and increase the faith — let the scent adrift.

I like essences in herbs, in books, in films — the kind that heightens the senses with the sensation of possibilities; of new answers; of new conclusions for old conundrum; of challenges to statistics altering probabilities. If I get up and go to the kitchen, cook fresh beans, forget the diet, and increase the intake of vitamins in order to influence, contribute and create something new — what will be, what might become.

I want to taste everything, discipline the body; avoiding excess, maintaining balance. I love cheese. Dinner feeds the immortal that lives in a mortal body; it makes the cells drunk with flavor and rhythm. Sensations are on the table — childhood, siblings, resentment, hope and passion.

To enjoy them, you need to be open; to absorb them, you need dedication. Explore with your mouth the chances of triumph; keep your anger at bay, it is not a good hand to play — you will need it to find your will, your speed and your persistence. Cut the meat, put down your knife and fork; and move on to the next battle. The fight is a blessing.

With no teeth, there is no nourishment. The sword

of the warrior is gone, the battles come to an end; and the age of diplomacy begins — the strategy of wrinkles handled with skill, wisdom and care, refined at every junction; knowing how to cook the facts; teaching how to transcend the moment, creating tomorrow. Gestures, limitations, words and silences — these are the seeds of an autumn that could still be good. Eat your mashed potatoes; mine, without lemon.

At my table, there is care, with little nothings and time. Raw or naked, pay attention — add reason when there is aversion, and use whatever spices you want. Your options may stain the tablecloth; leave scars on your skin — but do not remove them, because they are like pepper; those who do not ingest it are the ones who cannot digest it. To be outstanding, your options should be configured as niceties on the Sunday table — delicacies; the white dishes; the firm voices. Does everybody have to eat rice?

Please, do not use your fork to serve me. Save me a place and give me a slice. Share the home and leave room at the table. Everyone has their face, and I have my own taste. Why deny sadness? What if Mary were John, if Joseph understood Isabel, if the light went out and the land got drenched?

I am not you. I have other eyes, other words and other dreams. Who has the appetite for honesty? Truth burns, but it does not nauseate. Use your own cutlery. Put politeness on your lap and respect on your lips. Do not be mean. Use your napkin. Let bitterness go.

How often does the menu defy our sense of taste? I accept the challenge — recipes of sauce and words, confronting the herd mentality. To deny reality is to melt away the shield of emotions — to disturb an artificial, purposeless optimism. What comes next? Even with this awesome simultaneity, nothing is absolute. What is affirmed is that everyone is moving in relation to everyone else — destinies set in motion.

Sometimes it is necessary to flambé the discussion; to burn the compliments that cripple, reduce the will to overcome. Then the disagreement, full of obstacles, overcomes all. How many dreams are at the table? There is much love to put on your plate, please, make some room. When you are with family, call the priest, the doctor, the firefighter; impose respect.

I take responsibility for this work, on my own terms. None of that sick optimism that denies what it sees — indifference and waste; tastes and values ignored by those who cannot appreciate them; lives lived in different bodies — reversed tastes and shared digestion. Not even the power of thought and common sense can prevent certain acidity.

Can you pass me some tranquility? I want God, a home, a hero to guide me. I am not a saint, but I dream of peace and a little more silence — a dear partner that I lost between drinks, but will find again; with intelligence and a lot of effort. Could intelligence, for example, have ceased to be a guarantor of survival? I do not believe it. It feeds me and satisfies me. What a difference.

Today, I have scars on my knees and in my eyes; and an enormous appetite for life, as if I would never be reborn.

•••

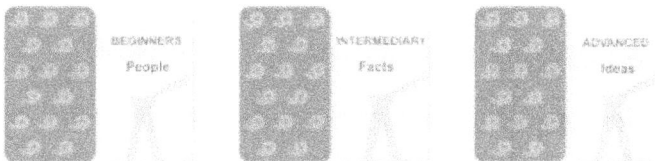

About people:

Who gets served?

Who moves around?

Who is a child?

Who chooses faith?

Who is a warrior?

Who writes the menu?

Who plays their role?

About facts:

What does it mean to be served?

How is the move made?

How does the child act?

How to choose a faith?

How does a warrior act?

What is on the menu?

What is your role?

About ideas:

How to be served?

What is the next move?

What kind of child do you want to be?

Where to put your faith?

When to become a warrior?

How to enjoy what is best on the menu?

What part of the character do you want to play?□

The Dessert

Dreams

I want to be big, like a layer cake; to fill the table and attract all eyes, provoking desire. I want to penetrate new territories through smell, stimulate the tongue, improving the sensations — step by step. I want to feel texture, to find in myself softness, to be as fascinating as sweets. With no excess, I want to have beauty and lightness; to be able to plant dreams and add a special touch. I want to create the moment and in an instant fulfill all expectations, inebriate the senses; leave behind a sense of longing.

The dream... Those who dream are like sweet angel food cake, united by the sugar — one is enough to satisfy desire, to give pleasure, a single dream come true eternalizing the dreamer. Try it. This could be your last chance. It is time to act. Do not let yourself go hungry. There is no reaction when the action has ended. Preserve life. Have more mercy, less disagreements. Long live the angel food cake.

I love looking at the Maraschino cherry, the absolute queen of decoration — a single one, on the top of the cake. While the strawberries, making a party of the filling, tell each other their adventures from the seed to the cake — they were planted, harvested, packed, carried, sold, bought, arranged into layers, at the table and in the world; even cut in pieces they are stuck together. They will never be alone.

Their fates are linked, on one side there is the dough, on the other the cream — isolated from the external world, they go on together, full of history, towards a common future. They serve the same purpose, and smile — an El Dorado in the middle of nothing.

In the happiness of not knowing, the strawberries play. Paralyzed by the joy of coexisting, they do not miss the landscape. How can you see what you do not know, if you cannot even notice its existence?

The cherry, on the other hand, belongs to the world. Alone, but integrated, it reached the top and lives up there. It sees the forks coming and going, and the big questions are unavoidable — will it have to face its inevitable fate from its throne? Being, at the same time, both purpose and end? Will it realize the danger of never coming down and never touching people, thus forgetting its own nature? How to make it all worth it?

There are those who prefer only to watch; and to be amazed with the colors, the shapes, the joy — a joy so great that it is enough in itself; eating is no longer necessary. They rest on the still cutlery of past opportunities, until the moment when they decide that looking is not enough, it is necessary to see. Seeing, they realize that there is a game in progress.

They decipher its rules, strategies, objectives, positions; and sometimes even the other players. When you get to this point, the game of life will never be random again. It becomes a system, governed by rules of behavior and reactions.

It is not easy. That is why we are not God, who allows us to systematize our lives and our world until we no longer want them, and go looking for change. All it takes to obtain the desired result is to acquire new behaviors. After this step is taken, we transcend our reality and go towards a new one. The ground disappears. The cutlery remains.

The jelly waits, like the wind, the hand, the spoon — consistent, flexible and transparent, discreet in its flavor and powerful in nutritive content; funny, slippery and clear, it strengthens the body that chooses it. It enchanted us once, when the world was funnier, and we used to slip into a reality that we believed to be clear and lucid; unlike the fascination a pie brings, with instant joy and lessons in power that not even the creamier cream could accomplish. Seeing the sky, though, is possible. Yes, I can do it.

Colorful, the sweets melt. Overflowing, they invite us to a celebration — dessert is free, like singing. At the table and in the streets, in the colors and the plans, they satisfy those who indulge.

The flavor brings memories of the grandmother, of school, of first love. When it happens, our enchantment is unforgettable, inebriating — it fascinates the soul. And little by little, the superficial layers are removed, the illusions are dissolved, until we get to the core, where the value is not lost; it remains impregnated in our sense of truth. But beware. Any excess is dangerous. A lot of ardor can be extremely painful.

I imagine hands that give shape; ingredients — strawberries, cream, jelly, favorable circumstances —

volunteers on the way, that in a single event seal their destiny as cake — to serve. And if you do not find them, mix, invent them — work and fate; all equal creations, so wonderfully arranged that no extra hands are necessary, whatever they have to offer — everything ready and stagnant, no gaps or flaws. Our reality is consummated; only the Creator can make it bigger and better. Should we say thanks? Just try.

With ardor or shame, savor it. Let yourself get totally involved, find the ecstasy and the despair. This capacity for wonderment, for a deep admiration of something we know but cannot fully reveal, gives us the real dimension of living. To deny the existence of magic is the same as to die; to limit the future and all its chances to what is seen, known and done — ignoring the new, the unexpected, hope. Give up jelly in order to shape the senses?

I prefer tasting; and to enjoy opportunities as I walk, while exploring new avenues of reality. Because there is emotion and enchantment, I sometimes need to contain myself as I sing — at the table, in pain, for love.

•••

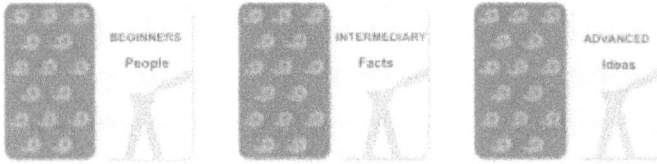

About people:

Who is a cake?

Who is a cherry?

Who is a strawberry?

Who is jelly?

Who is satisfied just looking?

Who wants to be great?

About facts:

What is a cake?

What is a cherry? What is a strawberry? What is jelly?

What can be satisfactory for one who looks? What is to be great?

About ideas:

How to be a cake?

In what situations can one wish to be a cherry?

What is the reward of the strawberry?

How to be fascinated with the purity of jelly?

How to satisfy oneself through looking?

How do you want to be great?

The Coffee

Transcendence

Today, I arrived water, but I leave denser. Those were intense hours, when I feasted in light. I did not waste my day. I relaxed my shoulders; spoke my mind; heard the coffee cups. I am ready to appreciate what comes next. With sugar, please.

The strong and the simple contemplated one another. In the heat of the moment, the coffee beans were ground, filling the transparent nature of the water with color. Mixed, they make their presence clear. Coffee, that marches and transforms, passes by and leaves its mark — on life, in the world and in dream. It learns to recognize an adverse nature; mine, his, yours. Consciously, the surrender happens, the encounter occurs — water and beans, apart no more, forever united in one drink.

Coffee has taught me two ways of assimilating

diversity — coexisting with the difference or becoming one with it. Amidst slow and quiet mutations, however, it is difficult to recognize the impulse to eliminate values; the tonality in music, the perspective in painting, the coherence in narrative.

Only when the process dilutes the existing certainties, frees unconscious dimensions and becomes truly consistent can innovation overflow — burning the day and marking the spirit. Old resentments and culture meld and revolutions happen.

Coffee stands alone, as do all powerful beings. Why is that? They stand alone because they are leaders, lonely and unique. They lead to a dream already dreamed, to a reality they no longer question; in their view, everything has become so clear. The better the understanding — of science, art and life — the more certain one is about the existence of something else, something beyond what is used at the table and in our relationships with others. Respect comes about by observing without judging and learning how to teach. These are notions and rules that widen the perception of what exists and mainly of what is ultimately important.

It is impossible, as with coffee, to separate the

elements that once were — until they were left behind to shape the future. What essence of power seduces us to the point where we transcend our being; to silence others and ourselves, to listen to our own voices, intimately, waking them up — in the solitude of passion, looking out the window, at sunset, on the lakeshore, at the threshold of knowing and creating? Bring on the cups, the mugs, the ideas.

I am ready to think. Ah, that whisper that disturbs me, begging to be heard, it insists on reminding me that it is necessary to see before the eyes grow weary. How many ears does one need to capture the cry, the song, the heart — the voices that haunt and those which soothe? I do not want, at any stage, not even for numbness, the impotence of disenchantment, the paralysis. It does not matter if I am too young or too old. I prefer the torment that urges me to action; living without leaving the baggage behind — or sitting on it, destroying the chains, enduring so much, almost suffocating, demanding space. I want more.

I long for that kind of calm that builds a fortress, a hug that makes a child feel safe. And as a child, guided by pure intuition, I free myself not to suffocate. While I relax,

I observe my adult self-taking control, laying down what it knows on the table, on the bed, on the grass, in some kind of meditation — dressed as rest. To make myself heard instead of leaving. The mature person in me wants to teach, to change, to exist — with no sound, no answer, no hurry.

But think carefully. It is necessary to cleanse that which is given to us, before putting it aside; to tidy up, to resolve, to dissolve the scents of the past, to make it resound with joy; not to leave the table like someone who — for an explicit lack of desires — projects in others what they love, to thank the sun and the moon; as for wishing on a star, choose for yourself.

I long for enjoying the greatest moments, those when you can feel the world, finding the answer; the sky enters the nostrils and the sea expresses itself in looks, its waves dictating our steps. It is a moment undoubtedly scented — it wants to intoxicate the senses, to inspire the next move.

Faced with doubt, it awakens in me the obstinacy of a scientist, instigating curiosity and envisioning other perspectives; intuitively, I leave to explore the world, having as companions the insecurity, some perplexity and a powerful imagination that transcends walls and rests on clouds. From there, if you are brave enough to look and have the mental acumen to be revolutionary, to watch the streets and observe the changes; to concede to mysteries, for they cannot be known, only sensed.

From a world that's yet to be, to expose the simplicity of the greatest — subtle and fragrant as coffee — taking a stand in the story you are writing. This understanding, unachievable in previous stages of the game, leads us to respect other peoples' life cycles; and in its transcendence, it prepares us for the next mystery, making life vibrant, alert to every form of love that wants to blossom. How wonderful the wisdom of life is. How is it not worth it?

•••

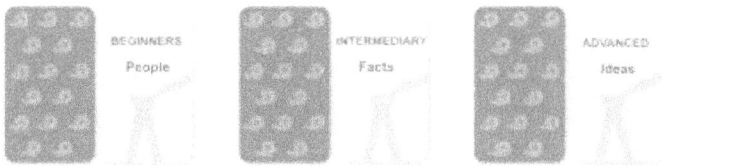

About people:

Who is strong in their simplicity?

Who is powerful and lonely?

Who is ready to think?

Who wants to change?

About facts:

What means to be strong in their simplicity?

What is power and what is solitude?

What means to be ready to think?

What needs to be changed?

About ideas:

How to be strong in your simplicity?

How much solitude can one accept to conquer power?

How to prepare the world to think?

What do you want to change into?

The Liqueur

Acceptation

I embrace the liquor; the proof; the whisper; the taste; and the calming I want to grab. Love and politics are on the table, passion on the faces, words in the air. The time for satiety is gone. Dinner is almost over. The spirit knows that continuing is necessary; it wants to stay — to keep warm.

The spark of life appears in the eyes of those who sat and feasted — they looked around and noticed their hands, the dishes, the humor. They assembled their lessons — the attachment to the tablecloth, the desire to perpetuate the moment; a work of love.

Liquor is art, a mountain to climb in the backyard. When we feel we have reached the end of the journey, a wonderful instant coming to an end or a great challenge approaching, art serves as a refuge — we seek the closest mountain. It is possible to climb it, to leave the weight behind, to escape the life that awaits us outside the door — to recharge our batteries and then reevaluate. Climbing the mountain removes difficulties, alleviates the unsolicited urgency.

Seen from the top, everything looks so small, malleable. Then we can expand our spirit and find our way — the right time to hear and talk. Let the discussion slide down our throats. Take a delicious deep breath; ingest the feeling of union, of passion. Surrender. Remember what has been said and repeat it no matter what. Hear the story again and again; and laugh, prolong dinner, the company and the moment.

For those who know how to listen, the spoken word will never be a waste. The more you listen, the more chances you have to resurrect a deaf ear, the movement of cars, the rustling of leaves. When you understand it is possible to do something different, you expand limits in such a way that even the words of a mute are made precious. Like an explosion, a train passing starts to make sense — history preserved in its windows. All that exists is infinite power, ready to be absorbed.

To be content with talking, hearing, being there; it

does not matter who says the last word. Beauty is in availability, in making yourself available. The fact is the discussion; the rest is merely words — to delay the future and savor the present; to remain seated, in a moment of eternity. Life is simply here. Now. Simple.

The best part is what has remained — to breathe, to remember, to live. The more you know yourself, the more you care about the knowledge that feeds you, the essential bubbles up, intuitively highlighted in the whole without the excess that blocks it. It exceeds; it alters taste; it makes you lose your touch — the point of it all. It is a precise measure.

This is the trajectory of the science of men and the work of God, enrapturing without maddening, like love, like moments of joy and pleasure — moments lived, remembered and commented upon; feeling wonderment and giving thanks; letting peace do its job, because the next conflict is at the door.

When the doorbell rings treat it with care; ask it to enter and listen to what it has to say — it is life, calling for the next battle.

•••

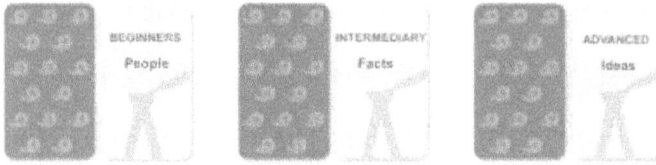

About people:

Who dominates the air with words?

Who climbs the mountain?

Who knows how to listen?

Who knows peace?

About facts:

What does it mean to dominate the air with words?

What is the nearest mountain?

What can be heard?

How to recognize peace?

About ideas:

How to dominate the air with words?

How to climb the mountain?

How to hear the answer of the world?

How to become a passenger of peace?

Amen

Almighty Father, today I chose to have dinner with You. I ask permission to enter this holy home and introduce myself. I've been very busy, I know, I have been absent. You see us inside and out. That is why You are my guest of honor every day, every moment — the shield that protects me, the light that guides me.

Thank You for Your constant presence, Your inspiration. Thank You for my health, my family united by love. Thank You for my daily bread. Thank You for my house. Thank You for one more night of sleep, for the capacity to dream. Thank You for one more day in this school of life. Thank You for hope, for intelligence — teach me how to use them; give me enough wisdom, so I deserve being called a work of God.

Oh Father, today I want to spend my Sunday with You. I want Your peace, Your balance. I want to feel that my whole being is involved in Your glory, getting ready for my mission here on Earth.

Everything I have is this will, and it will feed me. Make of me, oh Almighty Father, a great person — before Your eyes, and then, if possible, before the eyes of the world.

Give me the understanding that brings us closer to our humanity for we are often torn apart from others. And I know that those who have God, have everything. And there is nothing else.

Oh Lord, hear my prayer. You know me. Give me what I need today, according to Your will. Cleanse my soul. Set me free from my pains; give me the understanding to free myself from them.

This urgency will be my guide. Help me to be in the right place at the right time, and give me the necessary energy to learn and do what You need me to.

Lord, I do not ask You for power, but for the sensation of it, because this alone will unite me with my ideals and fills me with the strength to attain them. Keep me standing, to follow the path You have chosen for me. Great is Your power. Great is Your glory. Teach me to walk the path of light.

May Your joy be constant in our lives. Open our eyes to beauty. Open our minds for success. Your perfection will fill our paths, our lives, our souls.

May You provide us with abundance and fulfillment. May Your will be done. Today Lord, I want to have dinner within Your bosom. Amen.

Part V

The End of the Game

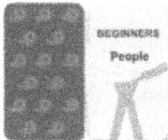
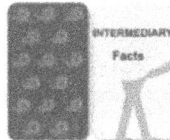

Score System

The score system makes use of specific criteria in each phase, according to each chapter's subject. The points you accumulate are not necessarily related to the moves you make, to the total amount of Sundays you experience.

Every time you accept the challenge and answer the topics, whether for beginners, intermediate or advanced players, you accumulate points. Your natural inclination connects you to people, facts or ideas. In order to score, you must add the corresponding aspects listed below. Familiarity with some themes might lead you to answer more questions in each section, increasing your perception of people, helping you to see facts that, if more deeply analyzed, may induce you to have new ideas — this alone is enough to make you a winner.

Every time you answer the topics for beginners, you develop a perception about the people who surround you.

You learn about their attitudes, the environment and how they affect you. Through the topics for intermediate players, you hone your objectivity, your analytical consciousness; and increase your ability to plan. Finally, when you accept the challenge for advanced players, you, a winner, gain access to the best life has to offer — the possibility of thinking, of writing, of innovating. You develop leadership skills and take the helm of this vessel full of people and knowledge which is your life. You maximize your score. You reach this point when you turn on the lights.

But who cares about the score, anyway? It is in fact a measure of your success. Being loyal to yourself leads you, the player, to the results you intended. This is your victory — to attain what really matters to you. Diversity and coherence mean extra points; they give the players strength and speed so they may pursue their goals, including a clearer and lighter understanding of the self. Victory is the final aim of the game; to win is getting what you want. This is the game.

This is your story, and the story of so many people around you — people systematically engaged, mixed with so many others and involved with so many things; people who wake up and go about their daily routine — full of thoughts, desires and pain, they walk, work, study, talk, listen and swear. Day after day, they control themselves; they control their voices, their words, their preferences, their strength, until the moment they can no longer endure. Sometimes, without even knowing, they let themselves be carried away. Influenced by the city, the countryside and the world, they build their families and coexist according to the consciousness they developed about life and living.

Add five points if you know how to define the stage you are in; and another five if you have not given up yet.

The ones who go furthest are those who see in the eyes of others what words cannot say; those who feel in the touch of aged skin the freshness of stories that tearful eyes hide. But many can only hear car horns. They do not perceive the instruments, the symphony of life, the scream of dreams suffocated in their chest. They lose the ability that children have — seeing truth in the eyes of others. They forget that tired and wrinkled skin is a consequence of the long roads travelled — delicious memories of our grandparents. They count the years by the calendar, leaving behind their own emotions and the plans they once made. They accept rules, but not people.

This is the game you learn to play as you evaluate the quality of relationships and identify the colors of emotions, retrieving from childhood forgotten possibilities.

Add two points for every memory you keep of your grandparents and two for every emotion you are able to feel.

There is so much to do. Our priorities guide us and we move on — sometimes advancing, sometimes only following the shore, the wave, the world. One day we wake up and realize it is Sunday. We do not need to go to the office. We can choose what to have for dinner. We surround ourselves with other people, other dialogues, and other silences. It is the moment to occupy our place in the family. We powerfully utilize every ounce of pain, every small fear, in order to sow our values.

Add three points for every detail discovered during Sunday's observation; and five if this detail refers to

you.

Each person has their own ideal; each person with their own family — some large, some lonely; at times noisy, other times silent. We are attracted and guided by our notions of family, our values, our idea of normalcy; our understanding of what is possible.

When you dislike a situation in the game, evaluate it from two different perspectives. First, you can run, run really fast to overcome the speed of the events and position yourself in the most advantageous manner. Secondly, you can use abstraction, mentally placing yourself above everything — in a temporary dissociation from reality, going a step further in consciousness and then evaluating facts, people and actions.

After you reach a conclusion about the steps to be taken, you can return to the primary context and then act. At any moment, it is worth repeating the same stage with a different strategy. Does the game ever end? With every new strategy, the scoring system can be altered. Once again you will be ready to change your shoes and listen to a new song, letting yourself be shaped by the masters who surround you, as if wearing your favorite clothes. You have personality, you are able to create.

> Add three points for each moral value transmitted by your family. Ideas and concepts that we carry and have not yet developed, because we have just recognized them, must be multiplied by five.

Everyone has a Sunday. Even when for some, Sundays only happen occasionally; once a month, or even on Mondays. Even when limited by our schedules and work shifts, everyone has their Sundays, and we can choose how to spend them; working, sleeping, crying, throwing a party, reading or going for a walk. We can also choose what part of it we will share with our families. Does everyone want to be responsible for their own decisions? To what extent do you determine your actions as a consequence of your beliefs in the Maker and the values you have adopted?

> Every activity done on a Sunday counts two points. For every habit you decide to eliminate you add three points and also for every new activity. If it is a collective activity, multiply by four.

There are families that are traditional. There are families that are chosen. There are families that are excluded. And there are families that are miserable. We feel that we are part of them; we are nurtured; we are wasted. They are like a magnet, with a powerful effect over each of us, whether we want it or not. It happens. It is time to recognize that. Moderation and objectivity are like pearls created by the awareness of current imperfections and of our own ability to get results.

There is a little bit of everything in the family; so many evils and so many comforts; so many traumas and so many examples of resilience. What do you choose? What do you look for in your family? What is the family you are in search of? The big difference between nations is how people relate to each other, their choices and their quests. Your attitude is your legacy to the world.

To score in the field of relationships, make a list of the qualities of a difficult person and count five points per item listed.

This is not about building a model, or a statistical

paper about wrong and right, hate and desire. A family is formed by living beings, mutant like us, constantly evolving. No one is complete, nor is anyone so incipient that we can shape them as we like. For your inner self to have profundity, be more than what others see.

Build your foundations in humbleness — not a servile humbleness with your head bowed, a prolix behavior of rehearsed gestures, but a feeling of humbleness based on an equality of the vital energy manifested in you and in all living things that surround you; in the contemplation of the beauty that overflows from your eyes and the eyes that see you; on the acceptance that this is not the final stage.

New rounds will be necessary for you and for others, like gods in formation. Each one acquires their own abilities, here and now; living with their imperfections, their equality and their development. Everyone is on their way, some for a longer time. They make their relationships richer through their eyes; through their stories — lived, suffered and learned, normally narrated with love — ready to pass them on to those who have the ears, interest and time. It is necessary to have respect for those who have been there, have done it, and now fill the house with their ancestral knowledge.

Count the rooms used on Sunday. Subtract the
bedroom. Add two points for each public place
and three for each private one.

Even if you avoid the game, you create a final result.
We influence and are influenced by our communities. If
you do not like the outcome, try to reevaluate your
attitudes, how you act in a given situation. Always analyze
your performance, but never accept being told who you
are. Only you have total access to your passions, your fears,
your pains and pleasures.

The truth cannot be anywhere else. The family we
see, we deserve, we support and almost always love,
expands to the workplace and the streets. The family is our
foundation, our safe haven; the family we meet every
Sunday, come rain or come shine, in pain or in sorrow.

The family awaits us on those Sundays when we
escape or draw closer; those Sundays that we hate or look
forward to; and those that change us, Sundays when we
wake up pliant, and others that we simply allow to pass, as
if we were frozen — these are lost days, but it is our

choice. It is our path. The greatness is in living the day in all its movements, words, sparks; in the setting of the table; in the sleeves rolled up to serve; in the social institutions; the cultivated plants; in the educated child — in the end, only the flavor remains. What else matters?

Who has awakened you for pain, for love, for life's energy? Which ingredients did you learn to use with your spouse, your father, your world? What matters is that you are ready to live.

Add five points for every new ingredient introduced in the daily menu. Adding patience or frequency will open new perspectives to your existence.

The player is immortal. What you do not complete today, you will finish tomorrow — if you want to, if you keep playing the game. There is an instrument for everything. You need to tune yours. Polish your objectives and improve your strategies. If you are sincere, you will make the perfect choice and awaken your senses; this will help you to advance in harmony with yourself, like the music of being alive.

Answers of beginners

I have worked a lot to be happy, which for me means to have moments of joy — to smile and to talk without worrying; to feel safety in the environment; to trust people and to let myself be embraced. I have understood what it means to receive, and by doing so, I have learned to give.

There was a time when the only thing I received from those around me was an embrace of the eyes. In some situations, this is all a human being is able to give, no matter how great the gratitude or respect. A kiss was just a memory, left in a safe world, while I travelled to distant zones. I embraced with my knowledge the few hopes of men, women and children.

With time, I managed to live with the despair of my impotence. I started to work with reality, even if it was precarious. And they noticed. The answer came vigorously. There were almost no protests or complaints. This resilience in the eyes of others started to be the only and extraordinary comfort that life had reserved for me. I have understood the life of the doctor — very often like working in a war zone or in underdeveloped countries, amidst a general scarcity. And so I have learned how to see a hug, a kiss, a look.

With every victory, with any sign of improvement, everything seemed to be magic, like a toast that breaks protocol. At that moment, what mattered was not the brotherhood or the act, but the little piece of God drawn on every single face, reminding us that there is something to celebrate, that there is more to life than cloudy days. There is also light and hope, God was present there; and I was thankful for being there, too, for being part of these accomplishments.

I have understood the life of the architect — changing the horizon with houses full of love, altering the skyline with energy, offering water like a balm and finding solutions for the general well-being. And so I have learned how to bring dignity to people's daily lives — to serve, to celebrate, to toast and to thank God.

Whatever your mood is, you can change it into a springboard for success. I do not know how to determine the mood. What determines the mood? Are the words said or the reaction of those who hear them? Sometimes, time seems stagnated before some affirmations; other times, what you hear has the ability of stopping journeys, paralyzing movements and reversing directions.

Where is the gift of determination, of grabbing the right moment and making history?

What is the essential component, the magic that magnetizes us and pushes us in a certain direction?

Maybe it is the tone, the sound of the dream, the dream of others which is also mines — the seductive word that sounds so powerful. I have understood the life of the politician — it is all about the specific tone; being precise, appropriate, and competent. Therein lays the power of listening, absorbing, collecting phrases, emotions and expectations to use them at the right moments, with the precision to reach our goals. And so I have learned how to determine mood.

Who has never had the world in their hands — the girlfriend, the parents, the world offered on a tray, totally adrift — depending on the decisions of the beloved, of their mood, their steps, their words, branding the skin with a hot iron, leaving a scar behind. This will never pass.

I have understood the life of the musician — turning the immensity of his feelings into a symphony; with every note, a character passes, but is not gone. He leaves a sign, a gesture, a mark in the eyes of those who have seen them — everything was recorded and coded, transformed into music. The intonation brings the action back to life, the connection, the value, even the love — and is never gone. And so I have learned the secret of immortality.

Others might change the subject, rehearse jokes or recount the news, but the question is who is reflected in the mirrors? I will always carry the scar. I have understood the life of the psychologist. I have removed the resentment from my backpack, but the disappointment remains — a residue is left.

Hear my plea. Look into my eyes, and show me that everything was worth it; that you made gold at the price of my pain; that at least for today, you know how to caress me, how to live. And so I have learned acceptance and sublimation; I walked with firm steps.

I arrived early and feel very hungry. I came to satisfy the needs that support me. Here I can be a child. I can be an adult, and I can be grumpy if I feel like it. You tolerate my brilliance. I have understood the life of the athlete —

while I protect myself the best I can, you still love me. I know that with discipline, with resilience, with obstinacy, you show that you love me. Now I have understood what matters. And so I have learned objectivity.

I have seen you admit mistakes, begin projects, meet people, set goals, sow ideas, mediate conflicts, calm yourself down, become infuriated. I have understood the life of the manager — searching for balance when facing the unexpected; preparing budgets for food, education and maintenance; taking holidays. In my eyes, you have always been capable, strong and powerful. And so I have learned how to do things.

In the contrast of colors, I have seen joy and movement. I have understood the life of the cook — it is in the onions, in the garlic, in the pepper; I have recognized his feelings in the meat, a veritable keep; I have discovered subtlety in sugar and discretion in coffee — a magician manipulating energy, making it come and go, working with his hands the nutrients that shape health, body and behavior. And so I have learned how to make choices.

The tablecloth is different, but the dishes are the same. The arrangement has changed, the sequence has been altered and the fuse shortened. Drinking water does not help. Only bread can compensate for the strong taste of pepper — our daily bread, shared to alleviate discomfort and bitterness. I have understood the life of the firefighter — breaking down barriers; setting fire to the core and reach the soul; shaking things up until the essence is rescued; adding spice in order to calm down; saving another from death in life. You are all pain. I have learned how it is necessary at times to forget yourself and seek another. And so I have learned mercy.

How much bread is necessary? How much water is required? How many people are at the table? Which divisions, subtractions and additions are necessary to satisfy all? I have understood the life of the accountant — it does not matter how much you have available; at the end of the day you have to pay the bills, find the balance and the right answers, or start all over again until you get there. And so I have learned perseverance.

At the entrance, there were always flowers; in the bathroom, always a soft perfume. The table was clean, and everyone was dressed for Sunday. I have understood the life of the painter — using his palette to determine predispositions; inaugurating smiles in order to establish a different atmosphere, favoring other themes, new recipes, opening doors, letting things flow. And so I have learned reasons to smile.

I eat salt to become noble. What is salt? It is a preservative that carries tradition; or a flavor that numbs the tongue and values proteins. What is salt good for? For emphasis. I have understood the life of the choreographer — working to awaken the senses and make life more beautiful, lighter, possible; pirouetting in between days, gesticulating among the characters of this dinner, this family, this reality that is my house, making sense, leading the way. And so I have learned how to make a difference.

Who lends a hand and brings the trays? Who arranges the cutlery; who serves equivalent portions, never equal — we are so different. And we want to have enough for me, for you, for them. I have understood the life of the lawyer — never holding justice in his hands, but using the cutlery to serve it with words that feed the processes of truth, mine, yours, theirs; enough to have peace. And so I have learned the relativity of human certainties.

Service and servitude are gifts to those in attendance, as in a party. There are rumors and discussions, a ceaseless coming and going. It does not blind you; just watch. I have understood the life of the waiter — smiling, they determine the mood; lending a hand, they establish possibilities; in handling the cutlery, they give what they have to give.

In their movements, I understand their offering which alters my trajectory — it is no longer only mine. Our gestures are intertwined and we move in tandem. Those who act also affect, correct, create. Those who accept, also amplify. And so I have learned reciprocity.

Some are faster, moving in unhurried speed; others with undisputed urgency. This is child's play, the rhythm of dreamers, of those who still believe it is possible that everything and anything can be done, needing only the will to make it happen. I have understood the life of the writer — his ideas; building stories; using words to compose the atmosphere, the environment and the characters; living the events they create, getting ready to generate effects. If you stop to watch, you will reach new conclusions; perhaps finding new beliefs, other values. You will recover your breath and run again. And so I have learned what childhood is made of.

There is a time to watch and a time to choose. Some prefer faith, and dedicate their time to disseminating it — more and more and more, everywhere, constantly. I have understood the life of the scientist — never wasting a fact when proving a thesis; full of certainty, making it manifest with examples from nature and mathematical evidence. He turns his life into a holy commitment. Everything he believes becomes an argument, a debate, a foundation, a construction. And so I have learned about revolution.

Never underestimate the power of the word; the power of silence, of spontaneous gestures, repeated and required — warriors in a battle against ignorance, starvation and the individualization of the human being. The potato is alive; it contains the energy of those who cooked it and the nutrients of the earth that fed it. I have understood the life of the teacher — giving lessons to a world in a hurry; seeing the other in another, other beings worthy of attention, deserving a word, a gesture, some recognition.

I have seen this battle at the table. I have recognized the moment, the exact cooking time. And so I have learned the meaning of respect.

We only take to the table what we harvest from the soil — the grain that becomes food; the leaf that got soaked with dew; the meat that follows its cycle and now serves as sustenance. The menu is the offering. I have understood the life of the farmer. I have understood the importance of choices, of abnegation, of care day after day — culture and health, generating a series of options, depending on the seed rather than chance; on interest; on dedication. And so I have learned the art of cultivating.

For every participant in the game, a role is assigned. Who is going to accept them? Everyone, with their desires, focused primarily on their own goals — orbiting around them while they have dinner. Take some respite. Work. That is the point — ironically, that is all there is. I have understood the life of the dentist — recognizing an objective and concentrating on it; in mute orbit, focusing on what matters most, treating that particular point.

He is the supporting actor who comes and goes, becoming eternal beside his dentist chair, transmitting the excellence of his profession. And so I have learned responsibilities; I have learned the detail, the routine, such as the habit of looking before acting — recognizing the situation, the table, the point of it.

In the cake, I recognize the family. No matter how much you travel, how many friends you make, there is always room for cake. Diets come and go and expenses are controlled. The family remains in the picture, in the memory, in the inheritance of gestures. We are the ones that make it, bring it or forget the cake. In this game, I am the leader. I am the cherry. I have eyes to see. And by seeing, I can analyze, put myself in any context that I choose. It is my moment. It is my game. With every move, I watch the consequences — the mother, the father, the aunt. This is my life.

In spite of all your certainties, there are always the others; the team on the field. Strawberries, somehow we are all strawberries. Born under the same surname, or almost, united by a single heritage, we remain connected by our beliefs, our fears, our ways of acting; disguised and hurt, but omnipresent — even miles apart, crossing other gardens, driving cars of different makes. In love we are one.

Jelly is what there is — values incrusted in the mind, shaped by the world surrounding us; the culture we live in; the education we receive. Depending on the rhythm, the model of the game might be altered. Everything is related to the steps we take, slow or quick. The fresher the jelly, and the life, the greater the flexibility; but also the frailty — that is why caution is necessary with the winds we challenge.

This is accomplished when you are vigilant. Caution

is watchfulness — a matter of beans on the plate, dishes in the cupboard, like people who have settled down, found their place and do not want to lose it, watching life as if it were a movie; it is all the emotion they are willing to endure. The notion of metrics has been abolished, in a possible translation of impulsivity; of someone carrying a soul ready for training, full of voids to be filled. Those who want to become great do not discuss it; they admire the unknown; they underestimate the unexpected.

They feel new shoes on their feet and want to travel, as though they were ready to fly, as simple as that. They remember love, strong and direct by nature, because love does not accommodate. It does not have empty spaces.

It approaches the world as a wind that blows and moves forward. It answers life with a lucid, clear and clean attitude. It is always circulating, it does not gather dust. It is powerful, lonely, perfect in its leadership; because to be a leader it is necessary to be ahead of everyone else; to foresee; to plan; to live the future in the present. There is no stopping, only needs to be addressed and an immense horizon to conquer.

So I have understood why the world is always ready to rethink itself, shaking off the structures established by history. To stop is to die; the world is a breath of life and renovation is the required answer. Oscillation is its march, balance its destiny. It wants to transform life into life.

Those who focus on themselves, ignoring the balance of others, aim to overcome obstacles. Going to the backyard, they open the gate and widen the focus of their attention. They have a glimpse of a context whose perspective is different than the individual perspective; and start to pursue it.

I grew up in this environment, involved in this energy that speaks, that dominates the air with words; that materializes what already exists in the mind, searching other lives for the resonance necessary to revolutionize — leaving the self, integrating the world, climbing the mountain, listening to the meditation. Who knows how to listen? Time teaches. It is all there — in the very bowels, it is a hint of the possible. Think like the universe, argue with life, and do not ignore the suggestions the world brings in peace.

Now I know. Peace walks hand in hand with prayer; the real journey is in reaching the summit, examining the nature of life. Peace uses time until it has climbed enough, step by step.

I am a successful professional. Coexisting with my family, I have learned the ways of the world and its nature. I have known admiration and contempt, pain and health; words that work. I know what not to do. I was brought up on people's laps, at the table and in the living room.

Now I am respected by my peers. People recognize my value. Life has generally rewarded my efforts. I have found enough to draw my game board. I had a mother, a father, brothers, sisters, grandparents, uncles and aunts. Some did not come in an ideal shape, but I had already learned how to play. I sought in the newsagent, the maid, the teacher, the driver, the examples that were not at the table.

With the natural authority of childhood, I manipulated the dice and filled the empty spaces. The use of memories is automatic, so natural, that sometimes I do not even notice how valuable the training was. I accept others. And when I really want something, I get it.

I agree with the training. "Sometimes, all you need to do is to want it;" and as you want it, you do it — failing and training until it happens.

Answers of intermediate player

For centuries, men have fought to satisfy their needs. It was difficult to be noble and delicate when one was hungry. But that was how the machinery worked. Success was born from will, from determination; from the persistence of reaching a goal.

This was how the world was changed. Men prepared the house, provided for their families, doing everything they could until they realized that even when the goal was not reached, they had accomplished impressive things. They had searched; overcome obstacles; gone beyond the necessary, the possible, in order to be able to smile.

The first masters of mankind were feet, hands and eyes — everyone learns from his own experience, according to their nature. Later, men described feelings and art; they confronted science and the nature of things, postulating individual identity, a unique way of perception. Exposing their personalities in the same way a kiss expresses the soul — first to please it, then to elevate it and one day, who knows, to liberate it, embracing its flight. Flying where evil becomes good like a flower that blossoms along the path of life, men evolved to soften their character, elucidating the art of living well for everyone who wanted to learn it.

I have listened to the wind many times. I did not know from where it came; what it had done; how much it had seen. I felt as if I was being born. Faced with my greatest anguish, everything seemed so small.

Before my soul, the soul that the wind served, I wanted to make a toast to the memory that the wind brought, to the eternal newness of the world, to the unimportance of pain. I want to go out and serve; to reveal thoughts and make them live; to thank God for the luminosity of the stars, as I interpose myself between feelings and things — the beauty of the world; I want to mediate conclusions in the hearts of men; and to practice, with caution, love and wisdom.

In this journey, the word has not always had sound. Science has many faces, physiognomies. Doctrines made an appearance. Philosophy analyzed the silence, captured the occult, the forgotten. Curiosity stayed in the room, stimulating the mind with memory and imagination. What the heart said was deeply simple, impressive, leaving a trace, determining the mood of those who journeyed to succeed.

Having lived well, they laughed often. They earned respect. Facing misfortune, they treated it as a springboard. They lamented, but persevered; they saved a soul that could only see the abyss. They fell, they got hurt, but never ceased to appreciate beauty, expressing their gratitude to the world with the most beautiful flowers. Looking for the best in others, they gave the best of themselves, drying the tears of both children and the elderly. Not everything that was created was perpetuated; some things were left by the roadside.

They were complete in their footsteps, in their words, in the seeds they broadcasted — now just memories, full of what they did, of what they sowed.

If there were mirrors, they would be witnesses to the images that appeared — of what was allowed to be seen. In others, there were clues; whatever you did not know, you could find in them. In friends, there was fulfillment. In thoughts, in poetry or songs you looked for joy, because all you knew was sadness; you looked for hope, the rose, because you only felt pain, the thorns.

Who would have possessed whom? Who produced the power, the tragedy, the flaxseed life is made of? The mirror revealed, and then cracked. It knew too much.

Why exist? Living was reason enough. Sometimes it would suffice that the days were there and that capital accumulated; because time is the true capital — to lose it is to ruin life. Through idleness, which means to be busy killing time or wasting it, in order to prolong it, we never notice that it is time itself that kills us. After a certain point, there was no return; it was necessary to yield to the hunger for living, doing, understanding — the hunger for growing.

To respect errors and as a result, to become stronger — the paths of science are built from mistakes, selected and refigured. This is what really matters, that everything happens in stages and we have to overcome them. Climbing is for the strongest. Only then can we reach a passage to the sea, to the fortress, to fulfillment; to freedom, like an immense desert — on the way, a renovation of realities, the strong scent of their presence announcing that movement, a pervasive feeling of life everywhere.

The footsteps and their owner never stand alone; facing the unknown, men and the ocean, attempting the impossible from deep within, attaining the possible, a resolute being at one with the world.

Admiring without effort what he could not previously understand, man has witnessed the development of feelings, of energy — energy that comes from the senses — and found a home in the mind, as music, floating, divine by nature. It has enchanted the soul, now elevated beyond its nascent condition, awakened by admiration and transformed by an energized atmosphere. Already incompatible with idleness, the soul understands that it is time to act like the light spirits; those who by nature are masters of their own will, often guided by consciousness. They are beyond hearsay. They are loved for what they are.

They have their foundations in love, provoking hate wherever compassion does not reside — a compassion that never kills, sacrifices or exterminates. Their love is borne of mercy and beauty — without thinking or calculation, a reason to exist; personality and attitude, an impetus; pepper to get up and go.

Living, perhaps; creating, always; action has always

been quintessential, the essence of intelligence — building what one wants, whatever it may be; dreaming the dream to make it manifest. Because through action, not merely existence, necessary progress will occur; for what does existence serve, if action does not seize the moment?

Castles were not built by fear or gardens by hesitation. It is only inspiration that amplifies activity, sharing possibilities and the search for pleasure. Pleasure was not disseminated without sensitivity — sensitivity sculpted from pain by the hands of love, crossing centuries, hand in hand with human destiny. It was sensitivity that eased the passage, illuminating the landscape.

It taught us how to smile; it gave shelter to our fears; it chose to emanate hope, to give beauty a space; an opportunity and room for the future.

We have survived pain and unloving times, like a bird singing in the rain. We held the memory of goodness, of morals — the salt of the earth as presumed by science — not a doctrine, but a credential, a guarantee of happiness, like a treasure, a kept secret. We digested the thought until a total clarity appeared — the highest degree of intelligible persuasion.

Men, who wanted to be worthy of visceral

happiness, served others to satisfy their needs — a hungry man is not free. Neediness infiltrates; first the body and then the mind, until the soul itself doubts, becoming silent — its very existence withering. The wisest among them were prudent, understanding the process. They knew how to get what they needed before any action was taken — any facts established, recognizing in themselves the first cycle of knowledge. Forced to play their hand, they studied the cards dealt to them by fate; and played them to their best advantage. They tried — and they endured.

They decided how to proceed; their next move. They set their sails. They changed their rhythms. They knew where to go, starting with small daily acts. They waited for the wind while strengthening their character and building habits, step by step, until they could visualize the completed staircase, that could not be seen, only imagined. This empowering act made the world turn, beginning with the plate.

Satisfied, they slept. With the trustfulness of a child, they laid down their weapons; sleeping gave them back their innocence — a wise defense of impotency. They knew that someone less worthy, or greater than themselves, never existed. Occult, latent, unable to perceive the natural magic of childhood — what sacred thing happened in the apparent impotency of sleep? A child, as in a game — natural inclinations made visible without the use of force.

With the opportunity to observe, they identified talents. Educated in silence, in examples, they discovered how much joy and love were given to them, how high they could fly — warriors. Defining their malleable character, they were ready to reveal themselves in the torrent of the world. Impatience awakened them, stole them away from paradise; and because of this same impatience, they could not return. It was necessary to mature and dominate their anxiety.

Instinct, ever present, has freed men from their waning interests — comedy and drama coming from thought, from personified conclusions. Only faith remained, always liberating, elevating peoples to the point where offense could not reach them, preventing them from being petrified by their own preconceived ideas. With an absence of movement, dismissing alternatives, they knelt down in the mysterious depths of their own beings, reconciling themselves with life, with individual affection, towards collective solidarity — the family, the nation, mankind.

This is the victory of faith. This is why warriors existed. From the lucidity of the Greeks, who felt too little and acted too perfectly, they advanced, developing an elegance of thought and persuasion. They learned to join forces; to deal with mundane problems, with daily routine, making an effort to reach their goals. Thinking was more important than doing — never forgetting the celebration, the harvest and the results. They developed a metric for fear, called it courage and used it with patience and humbleness. They ignored the chains and dreamed of the world.

Nothing was wasted. Everything contributed to the creation of the menu, to the choices. It was never sensible to despair, to eliminate possible combinations. Without a horizon, there is nothing to lose. The sensation is of possessing nothing. Discontented, forced to fight, they decided to set the table; to satisfy their needs and sometimes their ambitions — of the man, of the nation.

What mattered was to make things accessible, the pleasure in the use of abilities, the recognition of needs and the possibility of making choices — choosing what was best, for royalty and commoners alike. What mattered was tenderness — appreciated in pain, actually a partner of humanity; a piece of the cake, every layer, every beloved person, in a fierce fight.

The rest was the shadow of those who were aloof, not knowing the nature of others, of the self, following the common path supported by the dough, the community; until the next throw of the dice. But fortune was tired of always being kept in the same wallets, walking the same roads, obeying the same laws. Once its location was changed, landscapes, colors and movements changed as well.

Looking backwards, the cherry understood how to face human laws. But it could not negate the natural laws that carried it on its back until the summit. None of that was enough. It was necessary to look ahead, to make things worthwhile; to live with everything else that life encompassed — in death as in life, a companion in acknowledging nature.

Nature is colorful. It is full of lenses, luminosity, even if details would be enough. Sometimes, it treated as truth what was only suspicion; it threw into greatness those whose figures were small and magnified the facts, forgiving controversies that allowed for enlightenment. Tragedy occurred only where fear blocked the light; for at any given moment everything was equal, similar, in harmony, as in childhood — strawberries, leaves, shapes; until the doors were thrown open and light entered. Differences set facts in motion. Progress and morals proliferated. There was brightness and vibrancy where only charity reigned.

Under the light of ideas, something was saved. The meaning was understood. There was no consternation with the brightness, or with feelings, for greatness was created from amongst the crowd through independent decisions. It was kept simple, like jelly, in its perfect sweetness — clean, amorphous, without preconception, favorable to life.

Life was shown as idyllic; man was prone to emotions, susceptible to passions; in sweetness, able to capture essence and permeate relationships with it. In treating others as if they were what they could have been, man made them believe. Then the songs, the paintings, the poems, the respect, the gentleness came up. They made real what once was only possible. With beauty, man valued existence. The faculty of sight did not become tiresome; it allowed them to save lives.

This greatness has not always been understood. To be great is to be lonely. It is in the nature of greatness. Perhaps because of that, it has always walked alone. By feeling the sufferings of others, it did not increase or exclude. It was truly great, master of itself. It went even further, recognizing in the success of others its own, and applauded.

It made itself even greater, deserving honors not always received. With that, it avenged the valuation that time never questioned. It simply strengthened what was already consummated. These were incomparable people, unforgettable moments. This was strength; these were unexplainable facts whose strength was felt, but whose simplicity is not yet ours to decipher. Perhaps if we had listened more, answered our own calling, looked inside our own closets instead of relegating them to the shadows, we would have heard the answer, and freed ourselves from the search for others.

The power of elucidating our monastic solitude was in ourselves. Underestimating the ardor of the soul, we insisted on blocking the noise. Whoever knew this art could have crossed the threshold of pain and avoided many obstacles — abandoning old clothes whose cut no longer fitted, shedding the ideas that used the body to crossover. The pain was gone. Locations were visited; prejudices were rethought and reconciled, as was the fear of places not yet known. Whoever had thought had sailed — they were ready, they left the margins adopting instinct as direction; and saw the other side.

Thinking has altered the heading, perceived the momentum — brilliant or mad; inappropriate; perpetuating changes; facing external tempests; determining the time that was no more; it overflowed. Wisdom has chosen, has changed the world according to its own nature and its different nuances. Circumstances have determined options. Intimately calm and ready, a new year was born, without the mistakes of the last.

Making use of the word, the years were silenced. Silence hid the cruelest lies, a tactic in the battles where words have failed. The habit of thinking dominated minorities, though not enough to oxygenate the majority. Innocence was drafted, purity was manifested. Silence quieted the air, concealed the novelty that the word could not broadcast. Humanity has not always made itself heard; but having desired, it survived.

In moving away from what they desired, men were able to analyze it. Some dreams were gone; others, like bonfires, burned; still others were made possible. Tenacity, tolerance and sagacity, employed with care, bore fruit —

new fruit. Born from action, consumed in the shadows of obstacles and examined closely, they awaited the next summit. Redemption.

Goodwill was a powerful media. Starting with intuition, it generated studies that created concepts; that culminated in ideas; that produced the actions of heroic warriors and valuable weapons. Therein nobles laid down their shields; they are now old — great spirits, whose glory had not passed, waiting to be heard; insisting on the value of humanity, seeking to wake it up. Any inappropriate gesture reflected on those who made them, nullifying the essence of integrity.

History, arts and dreams have never ceased to inflame us, taking hold of our senses — life exists beyond the body. The more loyal we are to ourselves, the more success we will achieve; the more we watch the stars, the more we will remember what can be done. There is a moral law within each of us: The higher we fly, the smaller we appear to be in the eyes of those who remain behind.

At any of these steps, we were able to smile, disregarding the looks of others — for we were closer to peace. I am the family that sat at the table; the family that was nourished and became closer. I am last Sunday, the absent aunt, the yelling father. I am the road travelled; the consummated fact; I am wisdom, the knowledge of the ancients, the masters of the past ready to understand, to transcend. I am proven science; solved conflicts; finished arguments; the book that was read; the museum that was visited; the film that was watched.

I am not a novelty; I am the answer, served in different formats and packaging. I know your past. I know where your beliefs came from, your fears, the story of your love — a story that came this far within the family. Now, the game is in new hands. It is not for me to determine the moves, the play; but I will show you how to get there — the strategy. If the player knows what to look for, it does not matter the throw of the dice. I recognize all sides; in your game board, I am a partner, a helping hand; friendly shoulders you can climb up on, for I will support you.

Answers of advanced player

The smile tells us that here is a human being. He likes what is good, that which correlates to what nurtures him. You need only to water the seeds of affection, already germinating, to see them walk the world, distributing gentleness, returning every hug, look and kiss. This is salvation, for everyone wants to feel accepted and welcomed.

To hug, you need arms. To kiss, you need lips. And to see, you need eyes. But to give in return requires only a person of good will. It is only they who live life to the fullest; with joy, they serve, thanking God with a special toast for their own capacity — being and doing; serving and shining, like the hope of the adolescent, with the belief of those that can do anything; cheerful, confident, looking up at the sky, holding to the moment; freed from others and dressed in the deepest of authenticity. This is the vocabulary of love.

To live in empathy, placing yourself in another's shoes is to be versed in the language of the soul. Knowing how to listen to eyes; to see the words and to choose the moment, the theme, the tone. Being all life, exuding the most intimate of motivations, it liberates its essence in the air — it deals with words with the mastery of those who see. In looking, they express the hope of those who know. They are sure that everything is worthwhile.

One must bless the tracks one leaves behind; recognize the courage of those who need it; proceed in spite of all conversations — controversies, points of view, values or desires; one must wake up and go to Sunday dinners, in a constant trajectory towards one's destiny — glory.

Reflected in the mirror, the images demand mercy, especially with ourselves — frankly analyzing what we think, setting goals for transformation. In the mirror are the collected clues — where to start; what to alter; where to arrive; always remembering the reasons for each of the lines revealed, so you can be prepared. Overcoming yourself, you become whole — a winner in life, in the way your life unfolds.

How do you awaken your hunger for life? Shaking it

with all the strength your capacity for love can muster. Every person who feels loved is ready to fight for what is beautiful; for joy; for prosperity; for happiness. This is why all forms of art are important — different views of the universe; new approaches to reality, taking mankind to a world that reflects people's anxieties and still makes them feel included — with the same family, the same home, the same financial condition and especially with those who have discovered that they are normal, competent, powerful.

Connected to God, we become stronger, ascending ever higher, as many times as necessary; looking for answers. In the only real dimension of time, the present — far from the nostalgia of the past and from the hopes of the future, since both take you away from the real triumph — you reconcile with what already exists. Determined, we challenge fate and adjust our steps accordingly.

To open spaces, we become ambulant energy, an incandescent spark in the soul of the universe, filling everyone and everything. Like waves of realization, hope and peace, we stimulate people to influence the environment, using their time to create beauty and gentleness, in a virtuous circle of respect and satisfaction, without gaps or doubts; or war; or oppression.

Strengthening the resolve for this fight with pepper — strong and spicy — we awaken, through taste and behaviors that free lives and redistribute dignity. With solidarity, we oppose cruelty and gently counter what was only rudeness. In the family, we fulfill the empty spaces of individuality, as we monopolize taste and establish peace, without causing commotion.

Wherever we teach or learn, we must become necessary. To help or to be helped; what is the difference? In some languages, learn and teach is the same word — in teaching we learn; accomplishing all that we could not achieve by ourselves. In aggregating the possible dreams, we widen the advancements of the general well-being, setting free what is not yet imagined.

Now, after all the exaltation of individualism and the negation of established beliefs, it is time to inaugurate smiles. The case is urgent. How do we know whom to trust? The solution is in the family; its weight on its members' shoulders is immense. A family built on respect has the necessary values, and they can be exported to all segments of society. Mutual respect restores self-confidence, gives directions and sets limits. The solidity in attitudes dominates the environment; it is something to trust, a promising basis — it determines moods, becomes pervasive and attracts new adherents.

The players want salt, onions and garlic. They want meaning. They want a solid structure for their truths; principles to fight for. The demonstration is in history, in the family — the fundamental social link. With the weakening of rigor came marriage based on love, authenticity between couples — a novelty that demanded care and constant reciprocity. Having lost its position of dominance, the family changed, became more malleable, less rigid, a lifestyle.

Perhaps for this very reason, it is here that you find relationships that are not accepted on other levels, annihilated by ceaseless competition, by exacerbated animosity. Salt has found a refuge in the bosom of the family, sometimes in corrupted recipes. In the family, it is possible to find complicity, solidarity, most of all companionship — values that transcend the basic needs of survival. Only then does it makes sense to introduce spicy flavors, discussing victories, leadership, happiness; to honestly serve yourself, while respecting others.

Certainty and desire remain clear, as do the needs of all characters, all with the same preoccupations, the same joy, same difficulties. Naively, we believe they are only ours, but they are collective truths — parents love their children and children love their parents, an exercise in reciprocity, as education must be; reinforcing; deepening.

The anguish of the parents about the future of their children is like a compass. If applied to the social context, bingo. The planet is saved. It is raw material for responsible goals and attitudes — to be generous, lucid, prudent; starting from the beginning, the Sunday dinner, an example in life. Never before was love in the family permitted as it is today.

Cleaning is the right movement, illuminating, where society contradicts itself. On one hand it stimulates consumerism; on the other hand it laments the decline of its values. How is the question clarified? By consumerism, common sense, respect; testing innovations in the use of time; being calm; being correct; perceiving; recognizing what has value — the other, the food, the cousin; your health; your neighbor; politics.

Never ceasing to be that kind of child, whole, because it is with those we love that we can transcend and grow, achieving security, recovering the sense of existence. Children conceived in love are one of the safest conditions of a cure for society. A child does not invent what is right — beauty and love. A child discovers them as something bigger, that is a given. A child does not identify reason; it is almost a mystery to be assimilated. To give latent certainties to these little ones consists in stimulating, automatically, the actions of the next generation.

These are the children who can save the world; eradicate diseases; free us from fear; give life to different ideas; reproduce objectively learned behaviors and the values that surrounded them from the cradle; with ever increasing frequency — an explosion that can revolutionize the game.

Put your faith in your own family, recognizing in it the spark of the Maker; and live with this predisposition. The game is in progress. This is your team. Isolation is something harmful; it corrodes self-esteem, it sucks the marrow of success due to the lack of coexistence when you give up sharing experiences. Even with the brightest intelligence, with all our skills and talents, none of us comes close to the Creator, who allowed us to play the game and chose the teams —perfect for the function they were meant. Surrounded by our private universe, we forget the fact that all players need to be free; to accept; to change, to overcome and transcend.

Look at the women. Their historical experience is based in caring for the family, their social responsibility. Now, the skills acquired are a universal quest — knowing how to see, how to shape personalities, how to manage people for a healthy, promising coexistence; how to foster engagement, to project the importance of ethics in the souls of children.

At the same time, collective goals strengthen individuality and service, the care for others. Women have been doing this for centuries; caring for others are their mark — giving and receiving; the more, the better. Have faith. The parameters are good. Rediscovering your own family might lead you to balance.

Live with silence to become a warrior. Take rest, as someone exhausted after work. Listen to the voice of the environment and especially its soul. Understand your own reasons and motivations. Success in life is not success of life. Every life has a purpose; this is the unappreciable value of an existence. Success is to achieve it, whatever the financial gains may be. Silence changes perspectives, stimulates the senses; beyond what is known, seen, wanted. As a consequence, it becomes painful — insufferable for those who do not have consistency, do not build foundations, never took flight. It requires training and strength; it is a job for great warriors — seeing and understanding; thinking and planning and only then, realizing. Things will never be the same again — in the heart; at home; in the world. Wait. In the next opportunity, silence will give you the balance sheet.

Use what is best in the most polite way. Cooking with dedication is a deep form of donation — the workforce, the energy, the time; altruism. Take delight at the table. Enjoying what the world has to offer us is another story; the options are most assuredly presented.

The moment built constitutes the present. Be wise. No kind of love is ignored. Whoever it may come from, if genuine it keeps you erect, like the spine, carbohydrates and proteins. Know what is good for you; passion and pride do not understand it. Use your intelligence. Summon your self- confidence. Proceed with all the empathy you can muster and success will come, with any menu, under any doctrine.

Be the best part of yourself, the part that fits your talents and dreams, not the dreams of the world or the pockets of others, the reflections of others. Everyone knows what their destiny is, and admitting it makes it easier to endure. Travelling this road with determination makes the path lighter, saving energy that can be used in sports, pleasures, beauty; to strengthen and renew.

You want to be cake. How? Distinguish yourself as someone who has awakened, perceiving their own greatness and imperfection — deserving honey and cherries, arranging chairs, welcoming those who arrive. So they can feel your comfort, add strawberries with a lot of cream. On the game board, group them in equal terms, structuring them in a recipe that respects them; accepting; decorating.

In life, you wish to be a cherry, to be cheerful, to show gravitas in every situation. Look for the human being beyond the player, his connections with society in spite of his ethnicity, religion, culture. Forget the community bond; and by doing so, recognize yourself as equal, deserving of all rights. This is what makes the great leaders of mankind immortal.

The reward of the strawberry is to live in fraternity — communities. Companionship humbly puts us all at the same level. It is a great medicine for all pains, because as equals, we see our pains as normal. We carry our weight, with the awareness that the burden on our shoulders is similar and our brothers keep on going despite everything.

They choose consistence. They know the art of persistence. It fascinates them. It is like jelly; it explores human existence, designating a space for nature — to contemplate, to embrace, to educate; to learn; to enrich. Wait a little less and love a little more, escaping the trap of an unhappy existence, calming the fear of being really happy, on earth and in heaven — every moment at the right time.

Know your own dream. It is an option to lament the absence of what you do not have; dreaming of what others would do for you, or to you — of those who do not come and what cannot be. If we leave our dreams to others, they need at least to have the same dreams, exactly like ours. They need to make them come true, which makes their realization even more difficult.

Another option is using what you have, the presence of those who come; instead of despising them, with an endless wait for latecomers; taking over your own show, using your own hands, perhaps satisfying those who look after you.

You know how you want to be great, to grow, to

amplify the world; to overcome the way of looking at your family that you are addicted to; to expose the power of those who keep you chained to them, provoking you, forging you for life. They make you go and at the same time stay, never allowing you to leave home.

Repeating the pattern, we become our own parents, our bosses. Their march has revealed what is at the end of the path, but it does not have to be this way. Denying your permanent state of self-flagellation, saying no to depression, to starvation — the existence we disdain is the solution, a light, new alternatives. It is enough to look and choose differently, a happier end in the construction, more appropriate to our dreams. Make use of everything, of everyone, of the teachings of history, of the practices of modern life. Make use of your feelings, your skills and mainly of your will; starting from your home, your mother, the next person. Innovation is imperative.

In the simplicity that surrounds us, we perceive our intrinsic strength. Look outside, beyond the body, the backyard, the city limits; with this approach, use your intelligence to understand the work, the community, the politics, the planet. Reproducing externally what exists in the mind, the beauty of innovation lies in doing, in supporting well-being — becoming more, whole, by accepting a prescribed dose of solitude and letting others watch. Act, to conquer trust and clarify doubt.

This is how the world readies itself to think. Certainty is its foundation, and the detailed concretization of intention is your award — determining your route, powerfully leading you forward. How much life is your goal worth? How much time does your dream deserve? This is the price. You need to balance things.

With your own feet, climb a ladder, a mountain, your fate. Take as baggage whatever goes in your soul, in your mind. It does not matter the dimension you walk in; thoughts, soul, memories and dreams will accompany you. Words are said and consolidated; suffocated and dead before they are born, strategically thought to dominate the air; ascending through understanding. With coexistence, the path is chosen. To be travelled, the road must be understood, accepted, overcome. After all, what does the mountain, the corner of the backyard or the exhausting walk exist for?

Hear the answer, or be paralyzed. Lose at once the opportunity that is presented, forgetting the peace in your pocket. Miss the flight and fail. Become the landscape, losing your essence as a character.

I am the family that can do anything, in a game where love is the dice. The moves cause the solidification of values, the respect for the life you have, for the body you live in; for the food you take, the soil you cultivate. The strategy is the awareness of your duties and rights. Learn to walk consciously, knowing what you feel and what you make others feel — this is how a player is victorious, as well as the team called family, firm personalities ready for the torrents of the world.

They shorten the journeys, accessing human knowledge already available; applying it in their own community; acting with gentleness; respecting beauty, with humbleness and attitude. Citizenship is solidified through respect, love and actions. Players are the leaders of their own destiny, as far as their dreams can reach — beyond the body; the next person; the family; the faith. Achieving is possible.

Cooking for you

I love cooking for you, choosing the ingredients and mixing them. Thinking of you, I mix herbs, fruit and embarrassment; the secrets of the earth — wisdom, plants, flavors. My hands travel without a map, soaking the day in butter, milk and exercise. It is mystical, divine; it heightens the senses. I learn new ways and make others better. The recipe I prepare becomes even more delicious. Because you, I know, appreciate beauty. See my arteries; there is more than blood in them. There is hope.

The manicure goes as the scents come — onions, tomatoes, garlic. Hands tirelessly at work get warmed up; so does the soul. It is necessary to hurry, to get to the right point. Pay attention, or the moment is gone, but not the love. Love is impregnated in existence, in the vibration of pleasure. I turn on the music and think of you; music, work, energy and love. How beautiful a hopeful morning is, without myths, without fashion? Free.

Many items, many colors; tomatoes sautéing in the saucepan, dishes on the table, music involving the careful work, calling to the beating of my heart. I return to the mind full of you — cutting with my hands the precise shapes. Doing is critical. Proteins justify the gift, the talent, the ability of the food, laid on the tray and given to life. Acting is a renewal. A small cut and the blood comes, like a warning; and it soon stops.

The ingredients must be constant, as is the flavor and the freshness. I want to open your mouth, your nose and your eyes — with simplicity; without much fuss; without hiding places for the truth. This is why it is scary.

I want to inebriate with sagacity the pulsing life that awaits us; to awaken the unspoken words, the events that never happened. I want to fill your plate with dreams and your body with sustenance, with a lot of music.

It is necessary to have consistency when preparing the sauce, so it will be tasty and attractive, like the water we are made of — a lot of water. In transparency there is the brightness of those who have discovered love; and like a sauce cover the streets and go out into the world having children — unrestrained and powerful, the sauce changes and accompanies the dish. This is my allure dedicated to

you.

There must be rice, basic and special, with champagne, saffron or nuts. There must be a salad. And cheese, butter and olive oil — clear, dark and beautiful. One has to enjoy eating, and surrender to the delight of the senses — smell, touch; consistency; our first date.

I choose the food and lay the table — cutlery, serving trays and dishes. The mouth is served, between kisses and courses. It is the moment to open your eyes; before everything is over, before your appetite for victory is gone. It may security beat the will, inaugurating peace, passion and curiosity; and that special look of yours.

I love that look. In its threshold, I am certain that I could start all over again. I love you. I love having dinner with you. I love loving you. And those who know love no longer belong to this world. Love gives roots to a trace that is not conformist, but affable; that manifests itself in confidence, never in arrogance. And this makes us the owners of the world — discreet, they know they will get what they want; controlling whatever they do not want. Do not indulge. . .

The weekend comes, and with it another Sunday. I want very much to invite you to dinner. I want to wake up changed on still another Sunday — more awake, more lucid, more assertive. And if you accept, I will bring the board with me and challenge you to a game. You can choose the setting, the atmosphere and the participants. I will bring Q Tips for the ears and eye drops. As a precautionary measure, I will bring chewing gum for restless mouths and a little chamomile tea in case strong emotions are provoked. I want to see you picking jabuticaba berries with your hands, fill your hands with them, look at them — see them as possibilities. Act. Throw them in the air, against the wind, or with it. Chart the trajectory that you choose. Grab life with both hands. Live it. Roll the dice.

I will help you focus your efforts on what is really important — to reach the goals we establish in life is what changes human beings, brings them closer to immortality through their own realizations. And at the same time, tears them from those who walk beside them. This is today, when you already live what the future will bring. Are you ready to try? Would you like a cappuccino?

In life and in the world, I am looking for flavor. You cannot dismiss affection, a hug, a smile. And potatoes. Be authentic, simple. Simplicity is not a flaw; it is something pristine, crystalline and fundamental. The flaw is to opt for impotence.

I will remind you of the rules and go with you. Do not worry about what I think. To be understood by all or by no one — is there a difference between these two impossibilities? Freedom and individualism — two faces of the same coin that feeds imagination and stimulates creativity, freeing consciousness to do what are possible. To fly, even when everyone we love is still walking. Footsteps remain. Love lives on.

I will give you my best, in life and at the dining room table; for me, for my desire to see my beloved ones growing. Trust, be humble. Self-confidence and humbleness, together, can produce revolutions. Delicate and emblematic, they alter forms, words and wishes. They put all men on the same level of worthiness, and at the same time introduce reality and dreams —making them come true.

Friends, brothers, sisters, children, love; ah, love — a spice that absorbs, changes fight into pleasure. The satisfaction of discovering that the connections could never be treated differently is immense, understanding that the greatest step is to learn how to use them, with common sense and direction, for love's sake — to emerge from the cocoon.

Do not pay so much attention to difficulties, because when you overcome them, you will need to be ready for the next ones, much bigger ones. They will sharpen your mind, increasing your capacity for resilience, always leading you towards what you really want — to be, to fly, to amplify your perception of beauty, to see the opportunities presented to you; to search for the wind and celebrate life.

Embrace the air, perfume your words; every truth can be understood if we give it time and attention — blessing the mouth and illuminating the ear, until the music transcends it all and takes us to the Sun.

"Where there's life, there's hope."

Cicero

www.ingramcontent.com/pod-product-compliance
Lightning Source LLC
Chambersburg PA
CBHW051953090426
42741CB00008B/1375